The Dyslexia Assessment

The Dyslexia Assessment

Gavin Reid and Jennie Guise

B L O O M S B U R Y
LONDON · OXFORD · NEW YORK · NEW DELHI · SYDNEY

Bloomsbury Education
An imprint of Bloomsbury Publishing Plc

50 Bedford Square   1385 Broadway
London   New York
WC1B 3DP   NY 10018
UK   USA

www.bloomsbury.com

First published 2017

Library of Congress Cataloguing-in-Publication data has been applied for.
A catalogue record for this book is available from the British Library.

ISBN
PB: 9781472945082
ePub: 9781472945075
ePDF: 9781472945105

2 4 6 8 10 9 7 5 3 1

Typeset by Newgen Knowledge Works Pvt. Ltd., Chennai, India
Printed and bound in the UK by CPI Group Ltd, Croydon, CR0 4YY

This book is produced using paper that is made from wood grown in managed,
sustainable forests. It is natural, renewable and recyclable. The logging and
manufacturing processes conform to the environmental regulations of the
country of origin.

To find out more about our authors and books visit www.bloomsbury.com. Here
you will find extracts, author interviews, details of forthcoming events and the
option to sign up for our newsletters.

Contents

Part 2   **Curriculum assessment** 63

6   Assessment through differentiation 65

7   Assessment across the curriculum 77

Part 3   **Issues** 91

8   Social, motivational and emotional factors 93

9   Overlapping conditions 101

Introduction

We are delighted to have been offered the opportunity to write this book on assessment for dyslexia. We have been involved in assessment for many years and have therefore practised the ideas and assessment strategies covered in this book. We both agree that assessment is a process and that all personnel involved in identifying the educational needs of pupils and students have a key role to play. This also includes the role of parents, as they need to be fully considered throughout the assessment process.

Assessment for dyslexia can be seen as controversial principally because there is no single test that can identify dyslexia – a battery of tests and other assessment strategies need to be used. We emphasise this very strongly throughout this book.

We have attempted to make the book both practical and comprehensive. We have included ideas for assessment and intervention that can be readily utilised by teachers and integrated into the assessment strategies of specialists. We do see a role for both teachers and specialists in the assessment for dyslexia. The assessment should not be left to one individual. This again is something we emphasise in the book, especially when discussing gathering background information as well as utilising a range of assessment methods (see Chapter 4).

Furthermore, we emphasise the importance of early identification. This is crucial for a positive outcome for the pupil and we provide ideas and information on this as well as strategies for intervention (see Chapter 2). Furthermore, we acknowledge the role of differing cultures and the need to have culture-sensitive materials for assessing needs and diagnosing dyslexia.

It has been our intention when writing this book to give straightforward advice that will be useful for both professionals and parents. We hope to have cleared up some of the confusing elements that may arise in conducting and interpreting the outcome of a dyslexia assessment. In addition to looking at formal and informal assessment approaches, we also provide a focus on curriculum assessment in primary, secondary and tertiary education. We hope this book will be useful and will fulfil its purpose in providing clear guidance for conducting and understanding the dyslexia assessment and in developing appropriate intervention.

We would like to take this opportunity to thank the teachers, parents and other professionals – psychologists, speech therapists, occupational therapists and optometrists – who have helped to shape this book, and also those managing resources with whom we have consulted at conferences and other meetings. There are many very dedicated and specialist professionals involved in this field in both research and practice. This has been extremely beneficial in getting the correct information to schools and parents and has helped to inspire confidence in us all that dyslexia can be readily identified and appropriate teaching strategies and resources put in place. This can ensure a positive outcome for the young person with dyslexia. We sincerely hope this book helps, in some way, to achieve this.

Gavin Reid and Jennie Guise

Online resources

This book is accompanied by online resources including:

- printable versions of the questionnaires, forms and checklists provided in the appendices
- further details and weblinks for the various tests mentioned in the book that are accessible to teachers, specialist teachers and specialists
- an interactive, observational style index, which can be used when observing and identifying the learning style of a pupil or student.

Visit www.bloomsbury.com/reid-guise-dyslexia-assessment

PART 1

Dyslexia and assessment

1 Dyslexia and assessment: why, who and what?

Chapter overview

This chapter will:

- provide a working definition of dyslexia
- consider fundamental questions relating to the assessment of pupils and students who might be dyslexic, including:
    1. Why should we carry out an assessment?
    2. Who should be assessed?
    3. What should an assessment involve?

A working definition of dyslexia

We suggest the following points should be included in a working definition of dyslexia:

1. Dyslexia is a processing difference.

2. It is often characterised by difficulties in literacy acquisition affecting reading, writing and spelling.

3. It can also have an impact on cognitive processes such as memory, speed of processing, time management, coordination and automaticity.

4. There are usually phonological challenges.

5. It is important to recognise the strengths that can also form part of a dyslexic profile.

6. There will invariably be individual differences and individual variation.

7. It is important to consider individual learning preferences as well as the education and work context when planning and implementing intervention and accommodations.

The questions of why we should carry out an assessment for dyslexia, who should be assessed and what an assessment should involve will be explored in turn in this chapter, and are relevant to subsequent chapters in the book, although, as will be seen, they cannot always be easily separated from each other.

Why should we carry out an assessment for dyslexia?

One of the key reasons for systematically assessing pupils and students is because otherwise a sizeable proportion of them will not be able to achieve or demonstrate their potential. Every teacher will have come across individuals whose difficulties, and contrasting abilities, are clear to see. Anyone who has been involved in assessing will have also encountered a large number whose struggles, or skills, were masked in the classroom environment. So, assessment is often needed to uncover the individual's difficulties, and also his or her strengths. Both aspects are equally important if the individual is to be given appropriate, targeted support and the accommodations needed to demonstrate and improve his or her skills.

A methodical approach needs to be taken if we are to expect hard-pressed teachers to be able to fully understand and support pupils' and students' learning needs (see Chapter 4). A methodical approach helps to guide reflective practice, and to provide education that is inclusive and fair.

There are many reasons why individuals' struggles or skills are not obvious in class. For example, it is easy to categorise those pupils and students who seem generally less able, in terms of their literacy skills, as having *generally* low ability. It may be that they have not had the opportunity to show their talents because of the nature of the tasks they are given, how they are presented, or how they are tested in the general run of events (these issues are discussed in detail in Chapter 5). It is also quite common for individuals who know they have difficulties to avoid tasks they suspect they will find hard. We have all seen the student whose skills include changing the subject, making a joke, making trouble or delegating to his or her peers, or who refuses outright to carry out a task that should be manageable. Often, underlying this behaviour is a lack of self-esteem – with the added complication that this can express itself as the complete opposite! A pupil might have developed very good strategies for producing work that does not flag up any obvious difficulty but with the effort involved in doing this being hidden. So, for example, he or she might be spending much longer than you would expect on homework; there might be a bigger involvement than you would have envisaged from people at home; or he or she might be exhausted at the end of a school day with the effort of keeping up with peers. You could have a high-ability student who is working at an age-appropriate level, and you have no way of knowing that he or she could manage more demanding work, given the right circumstances.

There are additional factors that are likely to affect the individual's performance, and that can make it more difficult to identify dyslexia if there is no clear framework of assessment. For example, when a pupil or student has another diagnosis, it is often assumed that any difficulties are associated with that. So, dyslexia is not considered. Chapter 9 discusses overlapping conditions, such as attention deficit hyperactivity disorder (ADHD) and dyspraxia, which can have underlying difficulties in common with dyslexia. It is not surprising that some of the behavioural traits noted above are often believed to be the cause, rather than the effect, of learning difficulties. Similarly, cultural differences might be thought to explain different approaches to learning. It can be particularly hard to pick up the signs in students and pupils who speak English as an additional language (EAL). There is often an understandable tendency to attribute literacy difficulties to linguistic difference. This is discussed further in Chapter 10.

The importance of a systematic approach

We can see, then, that a systematic approach to assessment can play a key role in spotting dyslexic indicators that might otherwise have been missed. This is crucial, not only for pedagogical reasons, but also because it can enhance an individual's self-esteem and self-knowledge in relation to learning. An awareness of strengths, learning styles and preferences, and areas of weakness can form the basis for growth and development, both educational and personal. On a practical level, students can try out different accommodations to see how they will best be able to show their abilities in exam settings.

The individual pupil or student is of course the focus here, but it is also worth considering the rewards and satisfaction for teachers who see the results that systematic assessment methods can have on their students' performance and well-being. Parents, carers and family are also often grateful and relieved to know and understand the individual's challenges, and his or her strengths.

On a more general level, it is important that a systematic approach to assessment is supported by a whole-school ethos (likewise a whole-college/university ethos) that supports those who teach and support. This will also help to raise awareness and acceptance of the fact that some people work differently from others.

Early intervention

Early intervention is helpful because a primary-aged pupil is at the stage where key skills are still being learnt. It also means that it is more likely that support will be similar to work being done by the pupil's peer group; this can be important for his or her self-esteem. Targeted help at this stage can help to build the foundation for later learning, making it easier to access the curriculum and progress through school. It can prevent or anticipate later difficulties and provide a solid foundation for learning and teaching.

However, dyslexic difficulties are very often not recognised until later stages of education. This can be for the reasons that have already been noted. We often see, when the demands of school become greater, that a student's usual strategies are no longer sufficient, or they are too tiring to sustain. It should be noted here that the pupil or student is often not aware of using strategies to 'cope', simply because he or she is managing. It is reasonable to assume that younger children do not spend much time discussing their approach to classroom learning with their friends. When students do this in later stages of school, they can be subject to peer pressure relating to how long or how hard they will admit to working. So, just as the difficulties are not always apparent to classroom teachers, they are often not known to the individual.

Transition

The transition from primary to secondary school is often particularly challenging for students. More often than not, they will be in a different location, and possibly with different people. Students will have to learn to find their way around and organise themselves to be in the right place, at the right time and with the right equipment in what can at times be a busy and noisy environment. They have to get to know more teachers (and teachers will need time to get to know them). They will be working in additional subject areas.

The transition to college or university can be similarly demanding, with the additional challenge that students often need to be more independent and self-motivated. We often see students who are assessed as dyslexic at college or university – and sometimes not until postgraduate level – but who have managed to get to that level with no support. The volume and depth of reading, writing and organising in academic work naturally increases during these programmes of study. It is worth noting here, though, that some dyslexic students are better at higher-level, analytic work than they might have been at earlier levels of study that depended more on rote-learning. They are still likely, though, to have difficulties expressing their views in a structured way in writing, and particularly when under pressure of time.

Who should be assessed?

We have seen that there are a number of factors that can make it difficult to identify pupils and students who are dyslexic, and that we need a systematic and methodical approach to do this.

Part of this approach involves selecting who it is that should be assessed. This should be seen as an ongoing process, rather than a one-off screening exercise (although screening can play a role), and the nature of the process will vary according to the age and stage of the pupils or students.

Whole-school screening in early primary school

Ideally, all pupils in early primary school should be screened, because, as noted above, this would enable early intervention to be put in place that might avoid some of the problems that could arise later. There is also the advantage that primary teachers are trained in methods and means of literacy acquisition, and they might therefore more readily understand the rationale for the various formal dyslexia tests that are available. If dyslexia is identified and accommodated in the early years, it is more likely to become normalised in the classroom environment, and this can be beneficial to the dyslexic pupil's self-esteem.

It is crucial to bear in mind that screening tests (see Chapter 2, page 16) are not fully reliable. Just as it is important to identify difficulties at an early stage, it is also extremely important not to rule out difficulties because they have not been picked up at the screening stage. So, we can think of screening as a filtering process that can play a part in the identification of difficulties, but that should never prevent a pupil from access to other forms of assessment at a later date.

As noted above, pupils should not be omitted from the assessment process because they have been identified as having other learning difficulties, or because they have a different cultural background, or speak English as an additional language. Pupils whose difficulties appear to be behavioural or emotional should not be ignored either. Similarly, it is important to bear in mind that some of the pupils who are working quietly might also be struggling quietly.

Selecting pupils most likely to benefit from assessment in primary school and beyond

It may not be possible to screen everyone in the early years of primary school, and in any case, we know that subsequent assessment would be needed, even if whole-school screening did take place. We therefore need to have some means of selecting those pupils who are most likely to benefit from assessment (and this is another process that should be regularly revisited). It can be a good starting point to ask the pupil what aspects of school he or she enjoys, and what aspects he or she is less keen on. Even young pupils will often have some insight into their learning – what areas are hard and what areas seem to involve less effort. Generally, if a pupil is reluctant to take part in an activity this should alert the teacher to a possible difficulty. Parents and carers can be a very good source of information on how the pupil manages at home, and whether the child finds school stressful. It would also make sense to look out for signs in any pupil who has a sibling or parent identified as dyslexic.

Throughout school, and beyond, it is important to be on the lookout for 'difficulties, differences and discrepancies' (Reid, 2016) in the pupil's or student's performance. Pupils and students who seem to have more difficulties than their peers in carrying out certain tasks could be assessed. Those who seem to carry out tasks in different ways from their peers, even if they are successful, might need investigation. For example, this could include the pupil or student who talks through every part of his or her strategies while working, or who has to be reminded of every step of an activity before being able to complete it. Often, there are obvious discrepancies between the pupil's or student's verbal ability and his or her performance in academic work. When a very articulate and motivated pupil or student is unable to keep up with his or her peers, we need to find out why this might be happening.

The difficulties, differences and discrepancies that alert the teacher or tutor to the need to assess will vary with the pupil's or student's age and stage. A pupil or student might seem to have mastered the basics of word reading, for example, but might have problems with comprehension. It might come to the teacher's attention that the pupil or student manages well in certain aspects of mathematics, but has great difficulties in others. A pupil or student might be able to remember subjects that involve narratives (such as history), but find it extremely hard to remember subjects that have no obvious 'story'.

There are points in the pupil's progress through school where difficulties can be more easily spotted, making it easier to select pupils for assessment. As noted above, transitions from primary to secondary and beyond are particularly challenging. However, any major change in the normal routine is likely to disrupt a pupil's or student's coping mechanisms. This could include moving year groups, getting used to a new teacher or moving to a different room or building in the school. Moving to further or higher education will bring with it a different set of challenges.

Formal assessments will often draw attention to unexpected differences in a pupil's or student's performance – between subjects, or in relation to his or her academic work and verbal abilities. Difficulties noted at this stage should be swiftly followed up in order to avoid unnecessary failure and the clear impact this can have on confidence and motivation.

What should an assessment involve?

Assessment for dyslexia will vary according to the age and stage of the individual. Detailed discussion of assessment in the early years and primary school can be found in Chapter 2. Chapter 3 discusses assessment in the secondary school and in further and higher education. However, there are some key principles that should form the foundation for all assessments for dyslexia:

1. **Assessment should be strengths-based –** this is very important, because this provides the information needed to produce recommendations for optimising an individual's performance, which in turn is needed to improve his or her access to the curriculum. A strengths-based approach also helps to ensure that the experience is a positive and helpful one for the individual and those who are supporting him or her.

2. **Assessment has to be done with a purpose in mind –** this could be to provide additional, targeted support. For older students, it might involve looking at the need for study skills support, and exam accommodations. There must be a general goal to help the individual at his or her age and stage of education.

3. **Assessment should be seen as a process, and not a one-off event –** the signs of difficulties can be hidden; a very able pupil or student might have developed good compensatory strategies. In addition, learning difficulties can present in different ways, and what appears at first, for example, to be a behavioural or emotional problem might in fact be due to the frustration that can result from a learning difficulty. We therefore need to capture information over time and from a variety of sources. This links to the fourth key principle (below).

4. **Assessment should take account of a range of perspectives –** it should involve the gathering of background information from parents, carers, the pupil or student, his or her teacher(s) and others who have been involved in teaching or related areas. This could include tutors and healthcare professionals such as speech therapists, audiologists, optometrists, occupational therapists, psychologists and counsellors.

Formal assessment

Formal assessment is very useful in providing standardised measurements of the extent of difference between stronger and weaker areas, and this in turn can give some indication of whether the pupil or student might have a specific learning difficulty (SpLD).

A standardised measurement allows us to compare the pupil or student with his or her age group. However, we need to consult test manuals for information on test thresholds, and on the reliability and validity of results. Standardised scores should only be quoted when the participant's age falls within the age thresholds of the test. A test is reliable to the extent that the same results are likely to be obtained if the test were delivered on different occasions (and by different people), just as a ruler would continue to measure accurately over time. With tests, we can judge this by looking at their reliability coefficients. A test is valid if it measures what it claims to be measuring. This is fairly straightforward, for example, in a spelling test. However, if we look at reading comprehension, we can see that different tests are likely to be testing different aspects – including silent reading, reading aloud, reading and remembering (where the text is removed while questions are asked), reading for facts and inferential reading. This means that there is not one single reading comprehension test that will provide a valid measure of every area of comprehension.

We might also want to consider where the test was standardised – for example, with a UK or an American population. Generally speaking, it is advisable to use reputable tests that are recent and standardised on a similar population. There are some very useful tests that have an upper threshold of 25 years. These can be used with older students, and results can be analysed qualitatively. This is discussed more fully in Chapter 3 (page 31). The SpLD Assessment Standards Committee (SASC) has produced detailed and helpful guidance on tests that are suitable for the assessment of SpLDs (www.sasc.org.uk).

Informal assessment

Informal assessment can also yield a lot of useful information about the pupil's or student's learning styles and preferences, strengths and weaknesses.

The gathering of background information has to be carried out sensitively, particularly if no prior history of difficulties has been noted, and because those close to the individual might be unaware of any potential problem. Steps should be taken to maintain a good level of communication with parents and carers. If possible, a short, face-to-face meeting is often preferable to a letter or written questionnaire, because answers can be followed up if necessary on the spot. It can be useful to ask:

- What are the individual's interests at home?
- Does he or she like reading at home? If so, what kind of things?
- Does he or she like writing at home? If so, what kinds of writing activities are popular?
- Does he or she seem to like school? If so, what aspects does he or she like? If not, what areas does he or she not like?
- Has the individual had any difficulties in relation to vision, hearing, speech development or coordination?
- Does the individual currently have any difficulties in relation to vision, hearing, speech development or coordination?
- Does the individual seem excessively tired after school?
- How does homework go (in relation to the individual's willingness and ability to work independently)?

- Does the individual have any extra help or tuition outside of school?
- Has the individual expressed any views about his or her abilities? If so, what are they?
- Would the parent like any information from the school or college?

These questions may be given or discussed in the form of a pre-assessment questionnaire, a copy of which can be found in Appendix 1 (page 131). It is very important that the parents and carers should also have the opportunity to ask questions, and that they are kept informed of any further assessment that might take place.

The pupil could be asked similar questions, and these would of course be worded according to his or her age:

- What do you really like doing? What is it about these activities that you like?
- Do you like reading? If so, what kind of material (e.g. book, comic, magazine, newspaper, graphic novel, websites)? If not, what is it about reading that you dislike?
- Do you ever feel that words, or the gaps between the words, seem to move on the page?
- Do you often skip a word or line, or read the same word or line twice by mistake?
- Do you like writing? If so, what kinds of writing (for instance, creative or factual)? If not, is this to do with the physical act of writing, or is it the task of organising and structuring your thoughts into grammatical sentences? (It might be both.)
- How would you describe your handwriting?
- Would you prefer to handwrite or to use a computer?
- Do you like school? If so, what aspects do you like? If not, what areas do you not like so much?
- Do you find school is tiring?
- How does homework go?
- What do you think are your strong points?
- Do you have any weaker areas?

A copy of the pre-assessment questionnaire for pupils/students can be found in Appendix 1 (page 132). Other information can be gleaned from school records. This would include:

- attendance records – showing whether there have been prolonged periods of absence
- involvement of other professionals (for example, speech therapists, occupational therapists, psychologists, audiologists, optometrists, counsellors)
- school reports and records of support provided or planned.

If other members of staff are involved in working with a pupil or student, then their input would also be valuable. If a consistent approach is used, then staff members will quickly become accustomed to the format and requirements. A copy of the pre-assessment form for teachers can be found in Appendix 1 (page 133).

Informal assessment can start with observation of the pupil's approach to work. The following should be considered during the observation of the individual:

- Does he or she stay on task, or is a lot of prompting necessary?
- Does the pupil get lost in the middle of a task and therefore not complete it?
- Does he or she generally take longer than others to carry out the same work?

- Does the pupil seem to find it hard to remember information given verbally?
- Does he or she doodle or draw a lot while listening or working?
- Does the pupil prefer to work on his or her own, or to be in a group activity?
- Is he or she prepared, or willing, to read aloud?
- Are there particular tasks that the pupil avoids, rushes through or particularly enjoys?
- Can the pupil keep up with his or her peers in conversations and playground games?
- Does he or she ever seem anxious or tired?
- Does the pupil seem to be restricting his or her output to avoid making mistakes?

Informal testing in key areas can be used to indicate where best to start. For example, an individual's difficulties might be focused on a particular area of literacy, such as reading, spelling or writing. Within each of these areas, there might be specific aspects that he or she finds hard. It is useful to think of the different aspects in terms of foundation and subsequent skills. If the foundation skills are not secure, then it is likely that this will affect performance in areas that depend on those skills. It is particularly useful to explore not just what the individual can do on his or her own (static assessment), but also when provided with cues or prompting (dynamic assessment). This approach will still show where there are difficulties, but it is far more likely to also shed light on the individual's skills.

Reading

For reading, we depend on the ability to decode words, and this involves an awareness of phonics. So, if a pupil, for example, has never seen the word 'umbrella' written down, he or she might be able to decode it 'um – brell – a', and by putting the sounds together will then recognise the word. However, we can see here that the speed of decoding is important. The decoding could be competent, but very slow, in which case the word does not seem to emerge as a unit from the list of sounds read out.

It is also very important to stress that the English language also has a fairly large proportion of words that cannot be phonetically decoded, and these have to be learnt by sight. Importantly, a particularly high proportion of the 'first 200 words' (Fry, 2004) are sight words. So, we need to be aware of the fact that phonological awareness will not, on its own, help the child to become a fluent reader.

We have built up a picture now of the kinds of foundation skills that we should be looking at for reading: decoding, fluency and recognising sight words. If there are difficulties here, then it is likely that comprehension will be affected – although an observant assessor might notice that the pupil or student is using other contextual cues to guess at words when reading continuous text. Therefore, an investigation of foundation skills should involve looking at single-word and non-word reading.

Fluency can be assessed by taking note of the different strategies and types of approach used by the pupil or student. Does the individual hesitate, self-correct, apply phonetic rules, or avoid trying words he or she does not know? Timed tests can also be useful here.

In older students, we might find that foundation skills seem secure, but there are difficulties with comprehension. There are a number of reasons for this. It might be that processing is taken up fully with the task of reading and decoding – which would suggest that the student's skills are not entirely automatic. It might also indicate difficulties with either processing speed or working memory (cognitive abilities are discussed more fully below).

Spelling

Spelling similarly relies on knowledge of phonics to encode words, and also memory for sight words. A spelling test is the obvious choice of assessment, but it is very important to look not just at the score but also at the types of mistake that are made. Are the words that are written recognisable? Are they phonetically plausible? For example, a word with transposed letters is recognisable but might not make sense if decoded phonetically. Here, it is worth pointing out that some children who do very well in class spelling tests do so because they have rehearsed these words for that purpose. You will often see that if they are asked the same words on another occasion, they are unable to remember the spelling. Inconsistencies in performance are therefore an indicator of potential difficulties. For this reason, it is advisable also to look at spelling within a written expression test, and it can be very enlightening to see how being timed affects performance.

Writing

There are many ways that writing can be examined for potential dyslexic difficulties. It can be useful first of all to rule out problems that might be related just to the mechanics of handwriting. Some pupils and students find it hard to form letters evenly and consistently. If they have adopted a habit early on of forming them in a different way from the usual, then they are quite likely to find cursive writing particularly hard – because the joins are not always in the right place. This kind of assessment can often be done by careful observation of the pupil's posture and pen or pencil grip, and for certain age groups, standardised, timed handwriting tests are available.

In terms of written expression, it is important to consider the different elements that are involved. These might include grammar and punctuation at sentence level, and the wider structuring of an argument through the use of paragraphs and linking words or phrases. Spelling has been discussed above, but it is also important to look out for the repetition or apparent omission of words. These often indicate some difficulty with working memory or processing speed. Is the pupil or student using vocabulary that is at the expected level (for his or her age and stage, and/or in comparison to his or her verbal expression)?

Mathematics

Dyslexic difficulties can often be seen in a pupil's or student's approach to mathematics. Typically, there can be a tendency to misread the operator, so that he or she produces the right answer to the wrong sum. Worded questions are often particularly hard because of the reading and comprehension involved. An individual who has working memory difficulties will often have had great difficulty learning times tables, and carrying out mental calculations.

Working memory and processing speed

Mention has been made a few times of the impact that working memory and processing speed can have on the pupil's or student's performance. It is therefore important to consider these cognitive factors when assessing for dyslexia. Specific tests are discussed in later chapters (see Chapter 4 and case study in Chapter 5, page 51), but the effects of difficulties in these areas can often be seen in everyday performance. For example, an individual with processing speed difficulties is likely to take longer over tasks.

We often also find that a low processing speed is accompanied by a tendency to rush. It seems reasonable to conclude that this could be the result of always having to work quickly to keep up, and the habit then becomes difficult to lose.

Working memory difficulties often result in inconsistencies in performance, because it takes longer for the pupil or student to consolidate facts or skills, and for access to them to become automatic. A combination of working memory and processing speed problems can compound the difficulties. An assessment of cognitive abilities should also take account of an individual's verbal abilities and his or her visuo-spatial skills. This is where we will often find the strengths that help us to devise strategies that will help him or her to progress, as well as the weaker areas. Some indication of the cognitive profile will often also help to shed light on why that pupil or student is finding some aspects of school or academic work difficult. This can be hugely helpful in terms of metacognition (knowing about how we know) and self-esteem.

Summary

This chapter has provided a general discussion of the 'why', 'who' and 'what' of assessment. The next chapters in this section will discuss specific features of assessment for pupils in early years and primary school and students in secondary school, further and higher education, reporting on the results and implications for practice.

2 Assessment in early years and primary school

Chapter overview

This chapter will:

- highlight the importance of early identification
- discuss the factors that can prompt concern
- discuss the 'overcoming barriers to learning' approach to supporting young children with dyslexia
- discuss other signs of young children in early years or primary school being at risk of dyslexia
- discuss areas that overlap with dyslexia
- provide information on observational assessment
- discuss legislation for early identification.

Early identification

The importance of early identification of dyslexia was introduced in Chapter 1 (page 7). There is widespread opinion based on long-standing and current research that early identification is in fact the key to successful intervention. It is therefore important that teachers are able to identify those pupils who may either be close to failing, or show signs of being at risk of failing.

Reid (2017) suggests that early identification can be seen in two key factors:

1. identifying those pupils who have challenges with learning and literacy

2. monitoring and observing those pupils who appear resistant to intervention and as a result lag behind their peers.

It is well-established that early identification is really about raising concerns and does not necessarily imply that a diagnosis should result. It is also important to individuals who are resistant to intervention.

Identifying a profile

It is important to identify a high-risk profile that can indicate dyslexia. Indicators such as letter and sound knowledge, short-term and working memory skills, alliteration and rhyming abilities, speedy naming of objects, and sequencing, often along with possible difficulties, in accessing known words for objects, organisation skills and motor difficulties, should all be noted. With this information, a profile for the pupil can be developed and the main purpose of this is to develop an intervention plan to prevent failure. Early identification should have a preventative aim and not necessarily a diagnostic purpose. Early identification should therefore consider the pupil's learning profile and further assessment can take place if this profile of strengths and difficulties matches that usually associated with dyslexia.

Factors that can prompt concern

Many of the early identification screening tools do not diagnose dyslexia but rather identify children who are 'at risk' of dyslexia. An experienced teacher using observation and referring to the pupil's performances in the classroom can also spot the potential signs of dyslexia.

Below are some of the factors that can prompt concern and how these can be noted in practice.

Memory – forgetfulness

This can be observed and noted quite easily. It means repeated and consistent memory difficulties. This can be with following instructions, doing homework or relaying messages to parents from school or indeed when learning new rules. It is important not to misunderstand this for disobedience or any lack of understanding. It is very likely that when prompted the pupil will remember what has to be done but he or she needs those prompts first.

This can also be noted in remembering the letters of the alphabet and the sequence of letters of the alphabet and this clearly can have an impact on reading.

Familial history

A family history of dyslexia can give rise for concern and it can be reasonable to assume that there may be a risk of dyslexia. It does depend on other factors and this may not be a direct causal link but it can give rise for concern. The research is very clear on this. Molfese et al. (2008), for example, estimate that the risk of a son being dyslexic if he has a dyslexic father is about 40 per cent.

Much of this research has been focused on the heritability of reading subskills and particularly the phonological component. It pinpoints specific genetic regions that are implicated in dyslexia, and suggests that these regions can be responsible for different aspects of the reading and writing process, such as: reading and verbal ability, single-word reading, spelling, phoneme awareness, phonological decoding, pseudo as well as non-word reading and writing, language skills, rapid naming and verbal short-term memory. It is acknowledged that the impact of genes on learning and literacy needs to be accounted for but that one needs to be wary of studies that make sweeping generalisations based on genetic evidence. Nevertheless there is strong evidence that genes do have an impact on dyslexia and there will be children who are 'genetically at risk' of dyslexia. This point is important as it can provide pointers for early identification.

Coordination difficulties

These are usually associated with dyspraxia but they can also be an indicator of dyslexia, particularly in the early years – coordination factors can include bumping into tables and chairs and general difficulty with using space. The child may also have poor balance and fall over quite easily. Co-ordination difficulties can also be noted in tasks that require fine motor skills such as tying shoelaces, colouring in and drawing, as well as general writing skills.

Reaction time

There are a number of tests and subtests that focus on processing speed and reaction time. It is well accepted that reaction time and processing speed are principal factors associated with dyslexia.

Reaction time refers to the time it takes an individual to recognise what has to be done and then carry out the task. It is also similar to processing speed and this can be noted through observation.

The pupil might, for example, understand the task but take longer than others in the class to carry it out. Usually slow processing speed can be seen across the curriculum and in most classroom tasks.

Breznitz (2008) comments on the 'asynchrony phenomenon', which indicates that dyslexia is caused by a speed-of-processing gap within and between the various components of the word-decoding process. He also claims that dyslexic learners exhibit difficulties when transferring information from one hemisphere to another.

Difficulty concentrating on a task for a period of time

This is different from more general attention difficulties, as the distraction or inattention will likely be contextualised – that is, it will be dependent on what the individual is doing. An individual with reading difficulties will very likely be distracted or inattentive during a reading task.

Reading errors

It is important to try to identify a pattern of reading errors. This may lead to early identification but also provide some clues for developing an appropriate intervention programme. Patterns of reading errors can include the following:

- confusion between similar-sounding words, e.g. 'bush' and 'brush'
- confusion between words that look similar, e.g. 'tree' and 'trek'
- confusion between similar word beginnings and word endings (such as the words above)
- semantic confusion – this involves words that have similar meanings but are not at all alike, e.g. 'bus' and 'car'
- difficulty recognising phonological patterns in words, e.g. the sound pattern made by letter combinations such as 'ph', 'sh' and 'ch'.

It is also important to check for reading accuracy, fluency and comprehension and this can be done through silent reading as well as reading aloud, particularly further up the primary school.

Preparing an outline with profile indicators

It is important to prepare an outline of all the profile indicators you have observed, such as:

- Phonics – knowledge of letters and sounds.
- Memory – short-term and working memory skills (working memory involves holding two or more pieces of information in your head at any one time and undertaking an activity).
- Sound manipulation – alliteration and rhyming abilities; this can also be a test of articulation.
- Processing – processing speed; this can include the naming of objects or numbers.
- Sequencing – sequencing information, such as in a storyline or how the pupil carried out a particular activity.
- Play – organisational skills; this can be seen at a number of levels, e.g. organising materials for play, own possessions and personal items used in class.
- Familial factors – genetic component; as noted above this is increasingly becoming an important factor as more research becomes available on the hereditary aspects of dyslexia.

- Movement – motor skills difficulties and balance difficulties; these can often co-occur with dyslexia so it is important to observe how the pupil copes with tasks such as threading beads and colouring in pictures. You can also note how the pupil copes with climbing frames and outdoor playground activities.

An early years checklist could include a pupil having difficulties with:

- phonological awareness
- language, pronunciation, rhyming
- letter knowledge
- communication
- concept of time
- listening
- memory for rhymes, stories, events, instructions
- coordination, including being clumsy and accident-prone
- attention, including being easily distracted
- fine motor skills, including drawing, copying and letter formation
- eye tracking and the ability to converge from far to near
- establishing hand dominance
- balance, coordination and ball skills
- social skills.

The 'overcoming barriers to learning' approach

It is useful to view early identification and, indeed, the assessment process in terms of overcoming barriers to learning rather than through a child-deficit focus. In reality, information is needed on both the individual and the curriculum, as well as the learning environment.

The impact and results of the 'overcoming barriers to learning' approach means that all children would undertake the same curriculum, irrespective of the barriers that are identified. This approach indicates three steps:

1. identify the curriculum objectives

2. assess the extent to which the individual has met them

3. decide what action may be needed to help him or her meet the objectives more fully.

This action may take the form of additional support for the individual, but it can also be in terms of reassessing the curriculum objectives or refining them in some way to make them more accessible for the individual in order to reduce the barriers to learning that he or she experiences.

A key aspect of this is the monitoring process and this must be based on the actual curriculum attainments. The process can be extended to include:

- **What does the individual find challenging?** Details of the nature of the work within the curriculum that the individual is finding challenging, e.g. which letters does the pupil know and not know; which books can the pupil read fluently?
- **Why has progress been made or not made?** This investigative process is important in order to identify further curriculum objectives.

This type of approach needs to consider the pupil's classwork and this should be both comprehensive and detailed, otherwise it can become merely another type of checklist.

Whole-school responsibility

The importance of this type of approach is that the emphasis is on the barriers that prevent the child from meeting curriculum targets rather than identifying what the individual cannot do. This can be a whole-school responsibility as it is important that attitudes, targets and expectations relating to progress within curriculum access are consistent throughout the school.

Pupils who have challenges in meeting curricular targets are usually very sensitive and can find a change of teacher quite stressful. It is important, therefore, that there is a consistent view throughout the school on the challenges that might be experienced by learners at risk of dyslexia.

It is also important to note that early identification does not focus exclusively on 'within-child' deficits and these can often be apparent before the individual has had an opportunity to benefit from the learning opportunities in nursery or school.

The term 'early identification' may be more accurate if it were extended to 'early identification of learning needs'. This would be the first stage and once this is carried out then a formal assessment and eventual diagnosis may follow.

Other signs of being at risk of dyslexia in early years and primary school

Attention needs to be given to the possibility of a child being at risk of dyslexia. It is important that staff in the early years are familiar with potential at-risk factors, which include the following.

Reluctance to go to school or signs of not enjoying school

There is usually a good reason for this and it can be due to a number of factors, but difficulty with some aspect of schoolwork can be one of them. In this type of situation it is usually best not to force the issue but to try to find out the underlying reasons for this.

Handwriting difficulties

This can be a difficulty forming letters, or copying or even colouring in pictures. In other words, this can be anything that uses hand–eye coordination. There is usually a lot of pencil work in the early years and in primary school and if the pupil has significant difficulties with this it will impact on his or her self-esteem. It is best to deal with this sensitively as lengthy handwriting practice for someone who has a significant handwriting difficulty can be quite painful.

Poor organisation

This may be noted more clearly further up the school system, but it can still be evident in the early years and in primary school. This can include organising the materials on their desk or work area as well as what they may need for carrying out a task, e.g. for a drawing or investigation task. It can also include memory issues and forgetting equipment; it could be that the individual has not established a routine of bringing certain materials or equipment on certain days because of poor organisation.

Spelling difficulty

Once pupils are writing independently, spelling difficulties can become more obvious. Quite often pupils will be able to spell regular words such as 'under' and 'jump' but they have difficulty with word endings, e.g. omitting the 'b' at the end of the word 'climb'. Some words like the word 'guess' need to be spelt visually or the order of letters needs to be memorised, but it is easier for pupils to try to remember the visual configuration of the word. It is a good idea to look for a pattern of spelling errors. If a pupil is making a lot of visual-type errors then this can provide a lead into intervention. Irregular words such as 'comb' can be tricky as the 'b' is not pronounced. Similarly the word 'subtle', which has a silent 'b', is often misspelt and indeed misread. This can be particularly challenging for children with dyslexia because they have difficulty in acquiring automaticity in remembering the sequence of letters in a word and also in remembering spelling rules. This means they will show inconsistency in their spelling and will need a lot of over-learning to consolidate the spelling of the word.

The English language is of course very tricky, with almost twice as many sounds as letters, and some letter combinations make different sounds even though the same letters are used. For example, the sound combination 'ch' is used in the word 'chaos' with a different sound from in the word 'choose'. To further complicate matters, the sound 'ch' has two spellings: 'tch' after a short vowel as in 'catch' and 'ch' elsewhere. Other irregular words such as the words 'ache' and 'receive' are also tricky for children with dyslexia. These words are best learnt visually or using techniques such as mnemonics or catchy phrases (e.g. 'i before e except after c').

The Orton-Gillingham approach (based on multisensory, prescriptive teaching of the elements of language) and programmes such as *Jolly Phonics* (a child-centred, multisensory approach to teaching literacy through synthetic phonics) are very useful as they explore the fundamentals of the English language and pupils can become familiar with the rules, such as for short and long vowels. For example, pupils learn that only one letter is needed for short vowel sounds, e.g. 'at', 'red' and 'hot' and the double of letters as in the double 'c' can be used to protect the short vowel, as in the word 'occupy'. There are many rules like this in the English language, which need to be learnt or memorised. This can be tricky for children with dyslexia but learning the fundamental foundations of the language is a great help and this needs to be a priority for children with dyslexia.

Behaviour issues and resulting frustration

Dyslexia is often termed a 'hidden disability' because it may not be obvious. Sometimes, however, frustration and behavioural issues can result and the dyslexia difficulties can be overlooked as the behaviour becomes the primary issue. This means that a pupil may be referred for an assessment for behaviour issues, but it is important to consider that dyslexia may well be at the root of this and therefore it is important to investigate the underlying causes of a behavioural difficulty.

Overlapping difficulties

It is now well-established that many of the specific learning difficulties such as dyslexia, dyspraxia and ADHD can overlap (see Chapter 9). This means that it should be possible to plan to anticipate the types of challenges pupils with these difficulties will encounter. The following table shows the challenges that usually occur in dyslexia, dyspraxia and ADHD that can be noted in the classroom situation. Attention difficulties can also be seen without hyperactivity and this is usually referred to as ADD.

From the table on the following page, it can be noted at a glance how these three well-known conditions can overlap. There are two key reasons why noting this can be useful for assessment.

Fig. 2.1: Overlapping challenges: dyslexia, dyspraxia, ADHD and autism

Dyslexia	Dyspraxia	ADHD	Autism
Speed of processing	Speed of processing	Focusing on detail – may actually process too fast	Speed of processing
Literacy difficulties	Literacy difficulties and handwriting	Literacy difficulties	Literacy difficulties
Keeping on task	Keeping on task	Keeping on task	Keeping on task
Self-esteem	Self-esteem	Self-esteem	Self-esteem
Communication	Communication	Communication	Communication
Social skills	Social skills	Social skills	Social skills
Memory	Memory	Memory	
Recording information – expressive writing	Recording information	Accurately recording information	
Organisation	Organisation	Organisation	

Firstly, it is possible to prevent failure from occurring by anticipating these potential challenges and ensuring the pupils who have these difficulties are not placed in a position where they have to deal with new learning, which may be challenging in view of their difficulties. For example, if we know the pupil will have speed-of-processing difficulties then we need to allow more time for the pupil to complete the task. This should be recognised at the assessment stage; this underlines the importance of linking assessment and intervention. This applies to all the areas mentioned in the table above.

Secondly, one of the other reasons for using a table such as the one above is that it allows the teacher to note that there can be a significant overlap between these different conditions. This has been noted in the literature (Reid, 2005 and Weedon et al. 2017), which shows that often early literacy intervention and recognition of a pupil's learning preferences and specific presenting difficulties can lead into successful intervention.

The overlap – common concerns

It is possible to link assessment and intervention by focusing on some common aspects that a number of pupils can display irrespective of whether they have dyslexia, dyspraxia, ADHD or are on the autistic spectrum. Their needs may be very similar and this can have implications for identification and intervention. It is a good idea to identify a core of common concerns and to use these as a template for planning assessment and intervention. For example, some common concerns may be social skills, memory difficulties, recording information through writing and processing speed. These areas therefore can be tackled in a group situation, but the needs of the children with dyslexia, dyspraxia, ADHD and autism can still each be met using this type of strategy.

Auditory processing difficulties

Auditory processing disorder (APD) – formally referred to as central auditory processing disorder (CAPD) – can also overlap with dyslexia, and many pupils with dyslexia have difficulties with processing auditory information. This can be particularly relevant to the early years as they have not been able to develop cover-up or alternative coping strategies yet. The main issue with auditory processing tends to be due to perceptual or cognitive inefficiency or perhaps delay in perceiving, processing, organising or indeed responding to information that is heard via the auditory channel. This is different from attention as the pupil may well be attending and indeed hearing the information but will not be processing it! This can be noted in observation as in the framework below, particularly if it involves some peer or small group interaction. Although APDs are characterised by poor recognition and discrimination of speech sounds as well as confusion of similar-sounding words and also locating where the sounds are emerging from, background noise can make the situation worse for pupils with APD and it is important to get the environment right for optimum learning. For that reason it is useful to obtain some idea of the child's learning preferences through observation.

Observation framework

In the early years it is quite likely that observation will be more useful than traditional forms of assessment. This in fact is the rationale behind the assessment tool SNAP – Special Needs Assessment Profile (Weedon et al., 2017), which takes both an in-depth and a wide-angle view of the range of characteristics that can account for specific learning difficulties (see Online Resources for more information about this tool). But teachers can develop their own informal observation schedule using appropriate headings, such as:

- attention
- organisation
- social skills
- learning modality preferences
- independent learning
- writing skills
- number skills.

For each heading in this framework some key aspects can be included, depending on the purpose of the observation.

Linking home and school

It is important to note the role that parents and carers can play in early identification and assessment; collaboration with parents is essential. One of the important points is that a joint venture may be necessary between home and school in order to help the child develop a positive self-esteem. It is likely even with early identification that the child will have experienced some failure, even though it is important to ensure that identification takes place as early as possible in order to prevent the negative effects of failure being experienced by the child. The issue of homework and the need to ensure a balance exists between home and school are also important. It is therefore important that schools value each individual child and express this to the parents, and acknowledge the important role parents can play in the process of identification and intervention.

The links between home and school are crucially important as what teachers observe in school is only a small part of a much larger picture in that child's life. It is widely recognised that home plays an important role in young children's education (Reid et al., 2008). The home can be a source of support for the school and vice versa.

Some examples of how intervention can be carried out linking home and school are shown below for four aspects of school life: reading, behaviour, learning and social:

Fig. 2.2: Home–school links for intervention

Reading	Behaviour	Learning	Social
Paired reading with parent/carer	Joint home–school reward cards/certificates	Developing learning skills and strategies through discussion and guidance	Giving the child a voice – listening to opinions and supporting him or her in developing self-advocacy
Shared reading with other family members	Daily notebook with comments from both home and school	Homework and discussion of the type of homework that can be beneficial	Group work, after-school clubs, sports
Book clubs and shared magazines	Parent helpers in the classroom	Learning from board games and other game activities	Planned activities during family holidays and staying with friends

It is important therefore that parents or carers are involved in some way in the assessment process.

Hyperlexia

Hyperlexia is perhaps at the opposite end of the spectrum to dyslexia. The pupil with hyperlexia usually has good reading accuracy and perhaps a good visual memory and knowledge of factual information. But he or she will usually have a lower level of reading comprehension and will lack a real understanding of the text. He or she may also misunderstand instructions, jokes and innuendos and be unable to infer meaning from a passage of text. Such pupils may have difficulty in responding appropriately to questions on the passage and be seen as very mechanical readers – reading without emphasis on the key words. They may also have difficulties in understanding instructions – particularly if these are not 'straightforward'. It is important therefore to check for comprehension after each sentence or paragraph. It is also a good idea to ask the pupil if he or she can predict what may happen next and how the story might end. Inferential reading is an important skill in reading comprehension. To assess for inferential reading you can ask questions such as:

- What do you think will happen next?
- Why do you think she said what she did?
- How do you think...?
- What kind of person was _____?
- Why did _____ happen?

This will help to ascertain whether the pupil is reading fully or superficially. This is important to note as it can help in the planning of intervention.

The importance of early identification of decoding and comprehension difficulties

There is an ever-increasing desire to increase literacy levels and countries can be easily embarrassed by international studies and 'league tables' that identify those countries that are failing in literacy (Shiel, 2002). Substantial amounts of money and government intervention are common to attempt to secure a rise in literacy levels (Rose Report, 2006, Reid Lyon, 2004). On both sides of the Atlantic, in the United States and Canada and in the United Kingdom, recent studies have revealed that systematic, structured programmes for teaching reading can benefit huge numbers of children (Bell and McLean, 2016).

While it is important to appreciate that reading involves a number of different skills, both decoding and comprehension of written words are vital. If children cannot decode, they are unlikely to be able to comprehend what has not been decoded. If verbal skills are weak and the children have poor vocabulary knowledge, then even teaching the children to decode will not result in a high level of comprehension, so results on reading comprehension tests are likely to vary according to levels of oral understanding, not necessarily decoding ability. It is important therefore to ensure that early identification involves both decoding and reading comprehension. It has been noted above that children weak in comprehension but stronger in reading accuracy can be seen within the hyperlexia category and those children who are stronger in comprehension than in decoding may be seen as dyslexic. While these factors can be noted in a test, such as the Gray Oral Reading Tests – GORT-5 (see Online Resources for more information) – they can also probably be noted more fully through ongoing monitoring in the classroom situation.

Phonological processing

The research indicates that phonological processing is one of the main factors associated with dyslexia, particularly in the early years. This includes being aware of sounds and being able to manipulate sounds, recognising where in the word the sound is, e.g. beginning, middle or end, and recognising rhyming sounds. Children at risk of dyslexia will not be able to do this as easily as other pupils.

The Phonological Assessment Battery test – PhAB (Frederickson et al., 1997) – has a number of subtests that can be useful for assessing these types of difficulties (see Online Resources for more information). The items in this test can give an indication of the sort of points to look for in the classroom. These include naming speed, picture naming, digit naming and rhyming. These all apply to young children but those children who have 'slipped through the net' may also show signs of these difficulties much further up the school.

SEND Code of Practice

In England, the SEND Code of Practice (DfE and Department of Health, 2015, 5.36) makes a strong case for early identification and intervention. In terms of identifying needs, the legislation indicates that the following broad areas need to be considered for identifying specific needs (DfE and Department of Health, 2015, 5.32):

- communication and interaction
- cognition and learning
- social, emotional and mental health
- sensory and/or physical needs.

The Code of Practice (HMG, 2014) applies to all English state-funded nursery, primary and secondary schools, and requires schools to work with parents on a cycle of assess, plan, do, review. The expectation is that class teachers or form tutors will meet at least termly with parents to talk through the following:

- what we already know/have found out
- what we plan to do about it
- how we will update each other on progress towards it
- how we will know when we've achieved it.

This process indicates that early identification is more than a one-off test, as it involves a cycle of assessment and intervention.

In Scotland, the HMIE report (2008, p. 7) indicated very clearly that it is important to identify children's needs in pre-school and there was a commitment for educational authorities to assess children who were showing signs of difficulty in learning to read or spell – the idea being to tackle these difficulties before they become problematic.

It is important to note that early identification does not necessarily focus on 'within-child' deficits but must include the learning opportunities experienced by the child; the child may not have had sufficient learning opportunities in nursery or early years stages for one reason or another.

Summary

This chapter has shown that the value of early identification and early intervention is now well-established and many government initiatives highlight this factor. It is therefore important that there are the opportunities and scope for teachers to obtain the necessary training and develop the expertise to make early identification a reality in practice. This chapter has provided indicators that can prompt concern and information on observational development in early years and primary education. The next chapter will look at assessment that will apply in secondary school and in further and higher education settings.

3 Assessment in secondary school and in further and higher education

Chapter overview

This chapter will:

- provide an overview of general principles of assessment that will apply in secondary school and in further education (FE) and higher education (HE) settings
- discuss the characteristics of each of these learning contexts
- describe and discuss informal and formal tests that could be used
- provide a rationale for the importance of assessing cognitive skills.

Principles of assessment

In a broad sense, assessment for students at secondary school and in FE college and university tends to be oriented towards making sure that they have the right study skills and accommodations to fully access the curriculum and pass exams. That is, the focus tends to move away from changing the way that foundation literacy skills are taught and learnt, and instead to accommodating to that student's way of working, and to developing his or her study and exam skills.

In Chapter 1 (page 9) we looked at four general principles of assessment for dyslexia that apply across the ages. These were that assessment should: be strengths-based; be done with a purpose in mind; be seen as a process and not a one-off event; take account of a range of perspectives. The following additional principles of assessment are valid in secondary school, FE college and university settings:

1. Assessment should strive to create conditions that minimise effects of anxiety on performance.
2. The purposes of the assessment should be explained.
3. Formal assessment should be carried out in a quiet environment, with no interruptions.
4. Feedback should be given to the pupil or student after an assessment.

Minimising the effects of anxiety on performance

The pupil or student might understandably be anxious or tense, and for that reason it is very important to create conditions that minimise the effects this could have on his or her performance. This can be done in a variety of ways. The most important thing is to try to create a rapport with the individual at the start, and not to rush straight into formal testing. The tone should be friendly, respectful and professional – how this is achieved will depend on the style of the assessor, and the person he or she is working with.

Gathering background information (discussed in Chapter 1, page 10) provides a good opportunity to chat about likes and dislikes, to gauge the individual's demeanour and to find out about any particular concerns or questions that he or she might have. During the course of the assessment, it is important to note any changes in the pupil's or student's demeanour. Is he or she settling in, or becoming more nervous in some of the tasks? We have to think about conducting an assessment that is full enough to provide the necessary information, but bearing in mind that if the pupil or student becomes too tired, the results might not be a good reflection of abilities.

Explaining the purposes of the assessment

There should be some explanation of the purposes of the assessment, and who would have access to the results. This can often be a tricky area for younger pupils, who may not have been told why (or even that) they are having an assessment. Sometimes parents or carers express concerns about the pupil's reaction to a potential label. It might, on the one hand, make the pupil upset. On the other hand, it might be used as an excuse for lack of achievement. However, as noted in Chapter 1, an assessment should highlight the individual's strengths and show how he or she can improve. So, arguably, it leaves less room for 'excuses'. (Labelling is discussed further in Chapter 8.) It is therefore advisable to find out prior to an assessment if a discussion with the pupil about the purpose of the assessment is likely to be an issue. This kind of information can be obtained using a pre-assessment questionnaire, such as the example already discussed in Appendix 1 (page 131). In our experience, even when there are parental or carer concerns, it is usually acceptable to tell the pupil that the assessment will help us to highlight his or her strengths, so that if there are any aspects of school-work that are more difficult, we will be able to suggest the best ways of helping.

Students and pupils over the age of 16 should be asked for their formal, written consent to be assessed. They should also be asked to indicate who would have access to the results. For school pupils, it should not be assumed, for example, that this would include both parents. College or university students might be prepared to share the information with tutors, but they might not have considered it being passed on to work placements. Some discussion with FE and HE institutions on their policy here might therefore be advisable. A sample consent form can be found in Appendix 2 (page 135). Any form that is used should be read to the student, and he or she should be given the opportunity to ask questions.

A quiet environment for assessment

It is very important that formal assessments should be carried out in a quiet environment, with no interruptions. If distractions occur, appropriate action should be taken. For example, if the outside environment becomes noisy during an auditory working memory task, it might be best to stop for a break or switch to a visual, non-timed task until things have quietened down. This should be noted, so that it can be taken account of in the analysis and reporting of results.

Providing feedback to the pupil or student

Feedback should be provided to the pupil or student at the end of the assessment. It is not always possible to reach a 'diagnostic' conclusion, and in any case it is advisable to let the pupil or student know that further analysis is still to be carried out. Preliminary feedback should give an indication of the individual's areas of strength, and of positive observations, such as perseverance, motivation and creativity in responses. More often than not, the individual will already have some idea of his or her areas of difficulty. It is useful if some indication can be given of *why* these tasks might be harder. For example, if working memory is a weaker area, then that might explain inconsistencies in spelling, difficulties in structuring longer pieces of work, or an inability to learn times tables.

After the assessment, a detailed, written report should expand on what was discussed after the assessment, and it should include detailed and targeted recommendations for strategies, support and accommodations where appropriate.

The following sections will consider aspects of assessment that are characteristic to secondary school, college and university settings.

Assessment in secondary school

The secondary school environment offers both opportunities and challenges for assessment. These are related to the fact that there is a wider curriculum than at primary school, and that there will now be a larger number of teachers working with each pupil.

At primary school, it is likely that class teachers will have come to know their pupils quite well, and this can be helpful in determining whether, for example, an individual seems to manage better verbally than in written work. However, for reasons that are discussed more fully in Chapter 1 (page 6), there will still be pupils whose difficulties have not been identified. The transition to secondary school can put extra burden on pupils, who now have to manage a highly structured timetable in which subjects are taught in different locations by different members of staff. This means that difficulties might become more apparent. As more teachers will work with each pupil, so there are more perspectives on that pupil's work. The addition of new subject areas can give more information on the pupil's strengths and weaknesses, and whether there is a pattern that might indicate learning difficulties.

These opportunities for identifying learning difficulties do, however, depend on a number of factors:

1. A transition programme should be in place that would aim to identify and explore pupils' experiences.

2. Subject teachers would have to be supported and trained to spot potential indicators of difficulty.

3. Procedures would have to be in place for these difficulties to be reported and appropriately followed up.

4. There would need to be provision in terms of staffing and administration for someone to take an overview of each pupil's work across the different subject areas.

Often, Support for Learning staff will liaise across departments to ensure a comprehensive, systematic and coordinated approach is taken. It is clear that a whole-school approach is vital, because many of these factors will rely on the direction and support of management.

Another aspect of assessment that is particular to secondary schools is the need to comply with the regulations of external exam boards. Exam boards each have different requirements when it comes to providing evidence of the need for accommodations. It is important that the system and methods used in assessment take account of these requirements, so that if a pupil does need accommodations, there is more likelihood that the right level and type of evidence will have been collected. For example, if an exam board needs standardised processing speed or working memory scores as evidence of the need for extra time, it would make sense to include timed tests in the assessment.

Assessment in FE college

The population of students at FE college differs considerably and in important ways from that found in secondary school. It covers a wider age range, and will include many students who are returning to education. Most mature students will not ever have been assessed for learning difficulties in the past. Those students who have been assessed will often not have a copy of the results, or of the evidence needed for exam accommodations. Often, students have not had any support for learning, and unfortunately many of them will have had negative experiences of formal education. However, we also often see students at college who feel more motivated than when they were at school. This could be because they are now focusing on topics that they find more interesting, practical and oriented to the workplace. These subject areas are likely to attract a higher proportion of students who prefer a hands-on approach to one that largely involves learning and demonstrating knowledge through reading and writing. The students come with a wide range of skills and experiences, and the college environment often provides an excellent opportunity for them to demonstrate their strengths in a way that school perhaps did not. Many students will have responsibilities outside of college, including work and family commitments.

The college curriculum can be extremely varied, and some courses will involve work placements or other arrangements with employers or the community. These factors have to be taken into account when assessing students and recommending appropriate support and accommodations.

Assessment at university

The population of students at university is likely to cover a wide age range. It will include students who are returning to education, and increasing numbers who come from overseas and who might be EAL students. Mature and overseas students in particular have often not previously been assessed for learning difficulties. Those who were assessed at school might not have a copy of the results, or of the evidence needed for exam accommodations.

In order to get to university, students have had to demonstrate a level of academic success. However, a number of aspects of university life can present a challenge, and often difficulties will only become evident – or too much for the student to manage – when they get to this stage. Those who have recently left school will usually find that they are expected to be more independent than before. This relates not just to their academic work, but to more general organisational skills. This would include knowing which lectures and tutorials to attend, what preparation would be needed, and where to find materials (for instance in the library or for lab work). Those students who have been out of education for a while, or who have come from other countries or cultures, can similarly find this transition daunting. Many students will have responsibilities outside of university, including work and family commitments.

The breadth and depth of work at university can be challenging, and it is worth noting here that it might never have occurred to some students that they might be dyslexic. Many of them will, however, find it hard to keep up with the reading that they need to do outside of class, despite a good level of commitment. Written work involves progressively greater levels of critical analysis, and students with learning difficulties often find it particularly hard to structure extended written work. There is often a great deal of anxiety around exams. Some courses will involve work placements, and the implications of this would need to be taken into account when assessing for dyslexia and considering appropriate support and accommodations.

Informal and formal tests for dyslexia in secondary school, FE college and university

Reading

An assessment of reading should involve some consideration of the student's ability to recognise sight words (that is, words that are not regular and have to be remembered by sight), and his or her ability to decode words that follow the rules of phonics. We need to see whether the student has skills in these areas, and also if these skills appear to be automatic. For example, reading can be very proficient, but hesitant. A lack of fluency often leads to comprehension problems – at least on first reading. It can sound as if the student is reading a list of words, rather than continuous text that has meaning. Often, if the student is given time to reread a few times, and therefore to become more fluent in processing that passage, he or she will have no difficulties with understanding.

Informal testing

We can assess reading informally in a number of ways:

1. **Ask the student about his or her experiences:** Is reading enjoyable? If so, what kind of reading is preferred (e.g. fiction, non-fiction, graphic novels, comics, magazines, websites, newspapers)? If not, what is it about reading that is not enjoyable? Is reading difficult, or easy? How does reading aloud compare with silent reading? Does the student have to reread to understand the content? Does he or she have to reread to remember the content? Does the student experience any visual disturbance when looking at text? If so, it is useful to take a note of the details. Some people, for example, find that their eyes are drawn to the spaces between the words. Some find that the words themselves seem to vibrate, or move on the page. Does the student often miss out a line, or read the same line twice by mistake?

2. **Ask the student to read some text aloud:** It is a good idea to use a passage of text that is related to his or her programme of study, and that is at an appropriate level. A 'miscue analysis' provides a structured way of examining the different features that are important in an assessment of dyslexia. This would involve noting any hesitancies, self-corrections, failure to read words and tracking difficulties (e.g. missing or repeating a line). It is important when a word is misread to take a note of the type of mistake that is being made. For example, is the student misreading letters, finding it hard to read letter blends, or appearing to guess at words on the basis of their shape or the beginning letters? The misreading of letters might indicate some visual problems. Tracking difficulties are associated with unintentionally missing out or rereading words or lines. Difficulty in decoding unfamiliar words is often associated with dyslexia.

3. **Assess the student's comprehension of continuous text:** It is useful here to consider different types of question (e.g. ones that involve the retrieval of facts, and others that involve inference). Some consideration should be taken of the type of reading that the student is likely to have to do as part of his or her course. In exams, this would usually be silent reading, but for students of drama, for example, there is likely to be a large element of reading aloud.

Formal testing

Formal testing of reading should include the types of qualitative analysis described above. Test scores on their own do not provide sufficient depth of information for a full assessment. Formal tests should include a test of single-word reading, and many standardised tests are available. In single-word reading, there is no context to help guide the reader, and this means that difficulties are sometimes more easily spotted. Timed tests of word reading and non-word reading can also provide very useful information on fluency, which, as noted above, can have an important impact on comprehension on first reading. In addition, it is important to look at the reading and comprehension of continuous text. A number of tests are available, and the following factors should be considered when deciding which test (or combination of tests) would be most appropriate:

- Does the test involve reading aloud or silently? Reading aloud provides the opportunity for miscue analysis. Reading silently might provide a better indication of reading in exam conditions.

- Is reading timed? And, if so, is a standardised score for reading rate available?

- Is the content of the reading at an appropriate level, in terms of ability and interest? Some students who have reading difficulties might find that texts at their ability level seem childish.

- Does the test involve reading sentences, paragraphs or longer pieces of writing? Short sentences are likely to present less of a challenge to some students than longer texts. What kind of reading is the student likely to have to do?

Spelling

An assessment of spelling should involve some consideration of the student's ability to spell sight words (that is, words that are not regular and have to be remembered by sight), and his or her ability to spell words by following the rules of phonics. We need to see whether the student has skills in these areas, and also if these skills appear to be automatic. For example, spelling can be accurate, but hesitant. A lack of fluency often leads to problems with written expression. When pausing to think of how to spell a word, the student might lose the thread of what he or she was writing.

Informal testing

There are two main methods of assessing spelling informally:

1. **Ask the student about various aspects of his or her performance in spelling:** Is spelling difficult? If so, has this always been the case? Is his or her spelling inconsistent? Are there some words that are always a problem? Is spelling worse when writing under pressure of time? Does the student feel that spelling might affect his or her written expression? For example, some people might prefer to choose a simpler word rather than make an attempt they know will be wrong. What, if any, strategies does he or she use to help with spelling? Can the student spell phonetically? Is he or she able to use the spellcheck facility on a computer? Some people find that the words offered in the drop-down list look confusingly similar. If they choose the wrong one, this can make it very hard to follow the sense of what they have written.

2. **Look at the student's spelling in their written work:** When we do this, we should consider the following:

   - Does handwriting obscure spelling?

   - Are words attempted more than once?

   - What proportion of words are misspelt? It is important to note that dyslexic students sometimes make relatively few mistakes in their written work, because in effect their expression is limited to the range of words they feel secure in spelling.

- What proportion of words is not recognisable? This will give us some indication of whether the student's spelling is likely to disrupt comprehension for the reader.
- What proportion of words is recognisable, but not phonetically plausible?

Formal testing

Formal testing of spelling must include the types of qualitative analysis described above. Test scores on their own do not provide sufficient depth of information for a full assessment. Many standardised spelling tests are available. It should be noted if the student is particularly slow, or quick, to go through this test. Does he or she correct, or add letters in afterwards? Does he or she write the word in an unusual order? We are looking here to see whether or not spelling skills appear to be automatic.

It is also very useful to look at spelling produced in the course of written work. This can be done as part of a formal, written expression assessment. We sometimes find that students can spell when asked to in a test, but when they are occupied with the larger task of providing a written response, they seem to stop attending to the spelling. This is likely to happen where skills are not automatic.

Written expression

Informal testing

To assess written expression, we can:

1. **Ask the student about his or her experiences:** Is writing enjoyable? If so, what kind of writing is preferred (e.g. factual or creative)? If not, what is it about writing that is not enjoyable? Is writing difficult or easy? Are difficulties associated with handwriting? How does typing compare with handwriting? What feedback has the student had about his or her writing?

2. **Look at some of the student's written work**: An assessment of written expression should involve some consideration of the following:
   - level and range of vocabulary used
   - ability to formulate grammatical sentences
   - use of paragraphs and linking words or phrases to structure work
   - ability to address the requirements of the task
   - ability to stay focused on the question
   - register – some students use inappropriately informal language and constructions.

Formal testing

Formal testing of reading must include the types of qualitative analysis described above. Scores on their own do not provide sufficient depth of information for a full assessment. With written expression in particular, it is difficult to produce a score that is objective, because of the many factors involved in marking it, and the level of judgement that is required.

Note-taking

Informal testing

It is useful to:

1. **Ask the student about his or her experiences of taking notes:** Is he or she able to keep up when taking notes from the board? Is he or she able to take notes when someone is speaking?

Is the student able to read his or her own notes afterwards? Are the notes good enough to form the basis of revision?

2. **Look at some of the student's notes:** Check whether the student's notes are comprehensible.

Formal testing

Formal testing of note-taking should include the types of qualitative analysis described above. There are tests of the speed of copying text that can provide some indication of the pace and legibility of the student's writing when he or she is not also having to produce the content of text. Scores on their own do not provide sufficient depth of information for a full assessment of note-taking ability, because this also involves the ability to summarise information, often from an auditory source.

Numeracy

Informal testing

We can assess numeracy skills by:

1. **Asking the student about his or her experiences:** Is maths enjoyable? If so, what aspects are preferred? If not, what is it about maths that is not enjoyable?

2. **Asking the following questions:** These can be particularly enlightening, because difficulties that are indicated here are often related to a dyslexic profile:

   - Was it hard to learn times tables?
   - How does the student manage with mental computations?
   - Are long-worded questions more difficult than paper-and-pencil problems?
   - Are difficulties experienced associated with understanding maths, or remembering what to do?
   - Does the student lose track when carrying out long computations?

Formal testing

Formal testing of numeracy should include the types of qualitative analysis described above. Scores on their own do not provide sufficient depth of information for a full assessment. In Chapter 9 there is some discussion of difficulties – including dyscalculia – that can tend to co-occur with dyslexia. If the aim of a test is to see whether or not the student is dyslexic, or the impact that his or her dyslexia might have on numerical skills, then it is helpful to include a test that has worded problems, items that involve knowledge of times tables and multi-digit operations. It can also be useful to include a timed test.

Handwriting

Handwriting has been mentioned above in relation to spelling, written expression and note-taking. It is useful to take account of the impact that handwriting difficulties might have in these areas. There is some discussion of dysgraphia in Chapter 9 (page 106).

Cognitive profile

It is extremely useful to include in an assessment some indication of the student's cognitive profile. It provides three valuable sources of information:

1. **An indication of the student's reasoning ability:** If a student is dyslexic, then it might well be that the full extent of his or her abilities has not previously been discovered in school, college or university work. An assessment of verbal ability and of visuo-spatial skills might highlight areas of strength.

2. **An indication of the student's style of processing:** A cognitive assessment explores working memory capacity and processing speed. Difficulties in either of these areas are often associated with dyslexia.

3. **A fuller picture of the student's strengths and any weaker areas:** We can compare a student's performance across the assessment. For example, we can compare reasoning scores (verbal and visuo-spatial) with processing scores (working memory and speed) to see whether the student's style of processing might prevent him or her from fully demonstrating his or her reasoning abilities without appropriate accommodations. We can also compare reasoning scores with actual attainments to see whether the student seems to be performing below the expected level.

These comparisons are very useful in highlighting dyslexic problems that might not be discovered in an assessment that only examines literacy and numeracy. For instance, if a student appears to perform at a low but consistent level across these tests, it is often assumed that this represents his or her ability level; the student might be categorised in some way as a 'low achiever'. It is often assumed that students who perform consistently in the average range, or higher, have no difficulties. However, we could be missing the fact that this person could be performing at a higher level – or that maintaining an average performance involves an excessive amount of effort.

Cognitive comparisons can also shed light on why it is that a student might be having difficulties, and, crucially, what could then be done to help. If the key difficulty seems to be speed of processing, then clearly that individual will benefit from extra time to perform academic tasks. If working memory is involved, the student might benefit from study skills that will help him or her to understand, compensate for and develop in this area, as well as extra time.

Some assessment of the student's cognitive skills could be made informally, for instance by asking whether the student tends to run out of time in exams, or to take longer than others to complete tasks, and whether he or she has difficulties in remembering verbal instructions. Some students are very articulate and skilled in describing and discussing their learning styles and preferences, and this would give an indication of verbal comprehension skills. The student who prefers mind maps to written notes might have good visuo-spatial skills.

Formal tests of cognitive skills are available. The importance of comparisons has been pointed out, and when different tests come from the same battery, comparisons are likely to be more reliable.

Summary

This chapter has provided a general discussion of the assessment of dyslexia in secondary school and in further and higher education, and has described informal and formal tests that could be used in these settings. The next chapter will look at how to build a full and comprehensive individual assessment of dyslexia, and Chapter 5 will discuss how we report on results and implications for practice.

4 Formal and informal assessment

Chapter overview

This chapter will:

- provide detailed information and a general overview of the main factors associated with the dyslexia assessment
- describe the assessment process
- provide insights into the development of an assessment battery and an overview of the assessment process
- provide information on the rationale and selection of standardised tests, which are detailed further in the Online Resources
- highlight the links between home and school and particularly consider parent perceptions and the need for support
- acknowledge the importance of developing a plan for the barriers to learning and how these can be effectively dealt with in the classroom situation – this will then be discussed in detail in the following chapter.

The assessment process

The previous chapters have noted that assessment for dyslexia includes more than tests; it involves comprehensive insights into the student's learning. This requires a full and comprehensive individual assessment as well as a consideration of the environment and contextual factors. The dyslexia assessment is also a diagnostic process and therefore it is important to use standardised and formal modes of assessment as well as informal contextual assessment. As discussed in Chapter 2, informal assessment includes observation, curriculum assessment and ongoing monitoring along the lines of the graduated assess, plan, do, review process in England (DfE, 2015).

The example of British Columbia

There are similarities to the above systems in other countries and usually schools will have key personnel, or a school-based team, whose responsibility is to oversee the assessment process. For example, in British Columbia in Canada the school-based team consists of school-based personnel who have a formal role to play as a problem-solving unit in assisting classroom teachers in the development and implementation of instructional strategies. It also has a role in the coordination of resources for students with any special needs within the school. Additional information and measures may well be necessary, such as a referral to the psychologist for a Psych-Ed assessment, and the aim of this would be to better understand the student's strengths and needs in order to plan more effectively for that student (British Columbia Ministry of Education, 2016).

According to the British Columbia Ministry of Education, 'the purpose of assessment and evaluation is to plan and implement an educational program to help the student learn' (p. 24). This is in fact the main focus of this book: that assessment is not purely a diagnostic process, but one that must reveal information on the learner that will support the learning process for that student and at the same time inform teaching. The British Columbia guidelines indicate that assessment 'may include criterion-referenced or norm-referenced assessment' and 'systematic observation and collection of behavioural data to establish baseline/progress data' for the student and 'describe functional behaviours' that can have an impact on learning and teaching (p. 24). It should also include information from parents, student records and any other information that can enrich the assessment process, as well as interviews with students. This is a comprehensive process and ensures that the information is not totally reliant on standardised assessment and that gathering information on the student's learning profile and learning needs is a prime purpose of the assessment.

In the UK

In the UK, assessment for dyslexia can be carried out by an educational or appropriately quali-fied psychologist, or an appropriately qualified specialist dyslexia teacher. Class teachers also play a key role in this process. The purpose of this type of assessment would be the same as that outlined above in relation to British Columbia, principally identifying the student's strengths and identifying appropriate interventions that can support that individual. A diagnosis, if appropriate, can also be provided.

Also in the UK, an extremely useful guidance document has been provided by The SpLD Assessment Standards Committee, which, although aimed at students aged 16 and over, does con-tain useful information for assessing students younger than 16. They also have a sub committee: the SpLD Test Evaluation Committee (STEC), which reviews assessment materials on a regular basis and maintains a list of approved assessment materials for assessing SpLD in higher education (www.sasc.org.uk/SASC).

In the Republic of Ireland

In the Republic of Ireland, the Special Education Support Services (SESS) is indicated in the Dyslexia Policy Document (www.sess.ie/dyslexia-section/school-based-assessment), which advocates struc-tured school-based testing. In this policy there is an emphasis on both early screening and follow-up diagnostic tests. The points included in the diagnostic battery include the identification of compe-tence in specific skills in phonics, decoding, reading and spelling as well as auditory processing and motor skills.

The SESS document indicates that in the diagnosis and intervention of reading difficulties, it is important to ask a number of related questions about the issues that are causing the difficulty and the intervention that has been carried out and how effective it has been.

Data gathering

It is important that all teachers involved in assessment are familiar with the assessment process. This process can vary depending on the school and the availability of assessors and teacher assessors in the school, as well as opportunities for teachers to carry out diagnostic-type assessments. An example of this process should include the gathering of data from a wide range of sources and should not be solely dependent on test data. As noted in the previous chapters, some of the information should also come from discussions with parents and through observation in the classroom over time.

It is important to carry out observation and to be familiar with background reports as the degree of dyslexia experienced by an individual can vary according to the learning context. The dyslexic difficulties will be more obvious in some learning environments and contexts compared to other environments where it may not be so obvious. This means that observation can be very important as a means of gathering information on the learner, the teaching approaches and the classroom environment. If there is a lot of teacher talk, for example, the dyslexic characteristics can be more obvious, whereas if the focus is on discussion, visual learning and creativity, they may be less obvious. It is important that teachers and classroom assistants have a good awareness of the characteristics of dyslexia. A framework for assessing and identifying dyslexia is shown below.

A framework for assessing and identifying dyslexia in all settings

There are a large number of tests that can be used for assessment, and not all the available tests will be referred to or discussed in this chapter (a more detailed list is included in the Online Resources). The tests explored in this framework will, however, bring out the key points and characteristics of a dyslexic profile.

Sensory assessment

It is important to ensure that a recent hearing and eye test has been carried out prior to the assessment. This is important as there will be visual and auditory tests in the assessment and the presence of any hearing or visual difficulty can provide a misleading diagnosis.

Information from parents

This is crucial – parents have a considerable amount of information on their child and it is important that this is shared with the assessor. This has been discussed in previous chapters and is also discussed in more detail later in this chapter (page 43).

Word recognition test

It is also important that the assessor includes single-word reading. This means that word reading is carried out without the use of context. This actually makes it a more relevant test of decoding skills. When the pupil uses context he or she can guess at the word or use the contextual cues to read the word. It is important to obtain an idea of the pupil's actual decoding skills.

Non-word recognition test

This is perhaps a purer test of decoding as the words do not make sense so cannot be read automatically as perhaps might be the case in known words. In pseudo-word reading (non-words), the word has to be decoded so the learner has to have some knowledge on how to decode the word and also have some competence in phonological processing. The learner will need to know the word rules, e.g. silent letters and the sounds that groups of letters make when paired together. For example, in the word 'uncle' the pupil will need to know that the 'e' is silent.

Spelling test

It is crucial to include a spelling test as spelling can be very diagnostic of the difficulties the pupil may be experiencing in literacy. Spelling should be seen in a diagnostic way and although the spelling score is important, it is not the only useful factor to come from this test.

The Helen Arkell Spelling Test – HAST-2 (www.helenarkell.org.uk/shop/helen-arkell-publications/helen-arkell-spelling-test-hast-2.php) – is a good example of this (see Online Resources for further details). This test can be used by teachers, specialist teachers and psychologists and can be used with individuals from aged five years to adult. It also includes a separate diagnostic record sheet. This highlights the point made above that it is important to view spelling diagnostically.

Phonological assessment

This is important for pupils and students with dyslexia as a difficulty in phonics is usually the main issue that is causing difficulties in literacy. One of the most popular suites of tests in the UK is the Phonological Assessment Battery – PhAB -2 – for ages five to 11 and the PhAB, which caters for older children (see Online Resources for further details). It provides a series of ten diagnostic and standardised assessments that can be used to explore phonological awareness in children with reading difficulties. As indicated above, phonological awareness plays a significant role in children's development of reading and spelling skills. The PhAB helps to identify phonological difficulties, and once these have been identified, appropriate intervention can therefore be put into place. Some other phonological tests are discussed in closer detail later in the chapter (page 42).

Miscue analysis

This is a useful system for recording errors as the student is reading. The Gray Oral Reading Test (GORT-5) provides guidance on this, and this is discussed in more detail later in the chapter (page 43). Miscue analysis usually includes headings such as insertions, omissions, substitutions and reversals. Other headings can be used as appropriate. It is usually advised to record the individual reading and do the miscue analysis afterwards. It is a very useful system and lends itself to diagnostic criteria. This is useful in order to target intervention.

Reading/listening comprehension

It is important to obtain a measure of the student's reading comprehension and it is a good idea to use both reading comprehension and listening comprehension. If the individual has a reading difficulty then this will impact on his or her reading comprehension. If this is the case, then it is good to look at listening comprehension. This, however, brings auditory processing into account and this can also impact on the result of this test. It is accepted that the relationship between listening and reading comprehension becomes stronger after the child becomes competent in decoding.

Listening comprehension and decoding

The discrepancy between listening comprehension and decoding can also be used as evidence towards a diagnosis of dyslexia. Individuals with dyslexia would usually score higher in listening comprehension and have difficulty in decoding. Decoding involves word attack skills and, particularly, knowledge of phonological skills and phonological representations. Joshi and Aaron (2008) argue that listening comprehension is an appropriate measure for assisting in the diagnosis of reading difficulties. They developed the components approach to reading, which includes different key components necessary for effective reading – and listening comprehension and decoding are two key factors that contribute to effective reading. Additionally they argue that reading comprehension and listening comprehension are highly correlated, which makes this strategy worth considering. Aaron et al. (1999) identified three types of reading disability:

1. problems with decoding/encoding (dyslexia) but no listening comprehension problems
2. difficulties with listening comprehension (hyperlexia)
3. deficits in both decoding/encoding and comprehension (language learning disability).

While students with dyslexia may benefit more from phonological-awareness training combined with sound-symbol instruction, students with primary comprehension deficits would likely benefit more from teaching that emphasises vocabulary development and comprehension strategies.

Silent reading and oral reading

These can be quite different as pupils and students with dyslexia are often not too happy about reading aloud and they can score higher in silent reading. At the same time, with silent reading the individual may be more prone to waver off-task and lose concentration. This can be the case with children with ADHD. It is a good idea therefore to obtain measures of both reading aloud and silent reading. The Gray Oral Reading Test (GORT-5) discussed on page 43 is excellent for oral reading and the Gray Silent Reading Test (GSRT), which is untimed, can provide a measure of silent reading comprehension.

Expressive writing

This is always a very useful and, in fact, essential component in an assessment battery for dyslexia. It can be carried out in timed and untimed conditions and can give an indication of how the child structures written work as well as whether students are able to utilise their oral vocabulary in written work. This type of assessment should be scored for speed, content, structure, vocabulary and type of sentences (e.g. short, long, compound, etc.). There are a number of standarised tests that can do this, e.g. the Wechsler Individual Achievement Test (WIAT-II and III and the WIAT-II T) as well as the Test of Written Language (see Online Resources for more information on these tests).

Curriculum information

In many ways this is the bottom line, meaning that it is crucial to consider this! Is the student keeping pace with the curriculum, and is he or she coping with the work expected? Obtaining information on this is essential and it complements the test battery. Neither of these points on their own, however, is sufficient for a dyslexia diagnosis – both need to be considered. This type of information should help the assessor enrich the assessment process and this is also important for tracking progress at different time intervals.

Observational assessment

This should if at all possible be included in an assessment protocol. Students can perform differently in the test situation compared to the classroom. Quite often this is the case with students with dyslexia and observational assessment can provide useful data. It also provides an idea of how the individual performs and interacts with his peer group. Observation can be structured (formal) or informal. The important point is to obtain information that can describe how the learner performs in different conditions, such as undertaking different tasks and perhaps in a range of learning environments.

A closer look at phonological tests

The following are common phonological tests. All of the tests mentioned in this chapter are also discussed in the Online Resources.

Comprehensive Test of Phonological Processing – CTOPP-2

The Comprehensive Test of Phonological Processing – CTOPP-2 (Wagner et al., 2013) – is popular and used widely in Europe, the Middle East, the USA and Canada. This test can be used for children as young as four and goes up to aged 24. As well as identifying phonological difficulties, it can also identify specific strengths and weaknesses and can track and document progression – which is important in order to monitor the effectiveness of intervention (see Online Resources).

The authors of the test have placed the test within a theoretical framework that pinpoints three types of phonological processing relevant for mastery of written language:

- phonological awareness
- phonological memory
- rapid naming.

Phonological awareness

'Phonological awareness is an umbrella term that includes awareness and manipulation of speech at the word, syllable and phoneme levels. The ability to analyse and manipulate speech at the phoneme level is known as "phonemic awareness".' (Mahfoudhi and Haynes, 2009, p. 141)

In general, phonological awareness refers to an individual's awareness of and access to the sound structure of oral language. As indicated above, when discussing the Phonological Assessment Battery (PhAB), it is important to assess phonological awareness as this is seen as one of the principal difficulties in dyslexia, and studies show that children who are weak in phonological awareness display improved reading performance after being given intervention designed to improve their phonological awareness (Torgesen et al., 1997).

Phonological memory

Phonological memory refers to coding information phonologically for temporary storage in working or short-term memory. This is often referred to as the 'phonological loop' (Torgesen, 1996). Difficulties in this area can restrict a child's abilities to learn new material. Phonological coding in working memory therefore plays an important role in decoding new words, particularly multisyllabic words.

Rapid naming

The third aspect of the model underpinning the CTOPP is rapid naming. This relates to the efficiency with which young readers are able to retrieve phonological codes associated with individual phonemes, word segments and entire words. This is important as it has been shown that individuals who have difficulty in rapid naming usually have difficulty in reading fluency. Wolf et al. (2000a) found that intervention programmes that focus on fluency in word identification have been found to improve word-reading skills in children with reading difficulties.

Wolf et al. (2000b) have given considerable support to what is known as the 'double-deficit' hypothesis. The two deficits are phonological processing and naming speed and the rationale is that when both deficits occur together, the learner will have difficulty decoding words that rely on phonological skills and also experience challenges in quickly retrieving and converting the words into meaning. Bowers and Wolf (1993) suggest that individuals who have difficulty in both rapid naming and phonological awareness (double-deficit) will have greater difficulty in learning to read than individuals with deficits in either rapid naming or phonological awareness.

Research (Mahfoudhi and Haynes, 2009) supports the double deficit hypothesis and also includes a third group that have both deficits at the same time.

The CTOPP-2 therefore provides diagnostic information that can be used to assess the nature and extent of the phonological difficulty, but it can also be used as a measure of naming speed and also for monitoring and evaluating the learner's progress with intervention.

Woodcock reading mastery tests

A similar process to the above is used in the Woodcock reading mastery tests (Woodcock, 2011). There are three main areas to the model used in this test battery. These are:

1. reading readiness – including visual/auditory learning and letter identification

2. basic skills – including word identification and word attack

3. reading comprehension – including word comprehension and passage comprehension.

See the Online Resources for details of the age range for this test. This provides a comprehensive model using dimensions of reading that can lead to a diagnostic understanding of the individual's difficulties. Additionally there is a word attack error inventory that records the student's errors on target sounds and target syllables. This type of reading inventory is formal and structured. There is also some benefit, however, in using more informal measures to record precise reading errors, such as the system of recording miscues (see below). The Gray Oral Reading Tests (GORT-5) do precisely that (see below).

Gray Oral Reading Tests – GORT-5

These particular tests look at both bottom-up and top-down processes and are suitable for ages six years to 23 years, 11 months. They include the recording of errors in graded passages to obtain accuracy scores and timed reading for fluency, as well as questions on the passage for the reading comprehension component. Additionally, however, they include a miscue analysis system to record miscues such as meaning similarity, grammar, graphic-phonemic similarity and self-correction (Bryant and Wiederholt, 2011). This system can provide useful diagnostic information that can also help with planning.

Parents of children or students with dyslexia

As it has already been noted several times throughout this book, information from parents is essential to obtain. Reid et al. (2008) studied the impact of this and encouraged parents to participate in the development of a system for extending links with all parents. Reid et al. argue that effective communication is the key to unlocking confusions and contradictions that may arise between the needs of parents and those of the school. It is important that parents and the school have shared and agreed views on how to approach the child's learning difficulty and this includes identification and the use of terms and labels. Communication now is very often through emails and other electronic means. It is important for a number of reasons that this is supplemented by face-to-face meetings, but one reason is because some parents may not have computer access or computer skills.

Reid (2009) researched the views of parents of children with dyslexia in relation to their experiences with school communication. The information was obtained from questionnaires and interviews with parents in a number of different countries and it was interesting to note how parents' experiences differed – even among those parents living in the same areas.

Additionally, parents can experience anxieties throughout the process of assessment and identification. They usually will have to attend formal meetings that can be a stressful and perhaps intimidating experience for them. Additionally they may have to assert their views when it is not in their nature to be assertive. There are now quite a number of support networks to assist parents – often arranged through dyslexia associations or parents advocacy support groups.

Nevertheless it is important that professionals recognise that this can be an anxious time for parents and understand the need to ensure that parental anxieties are kept to a minimum. Overall the main concerns shared by parents are:

- maintaining their child's self-esteem
- assisting their child with new work when he or she has not consolidated previous work
- protecting the dignity of their child when dealing with professionals/therapists
- helping their child become organised and assisting with routines and homework
- dealing with peer insensitivity – this is not always common but it was noted by a number of parents

There is evidence that schools have launched programmes that can deal with differences and the notion of disabilities. Additionally there are a number of community and government organisations in many countries that can assist with this. Enable Scotland, which is a charity that campaigns to fight discrimination and inequality and ensure that people who have learning disabilities are regarded as equal members of society, is one such organisation. Although this organisation does not focus on dyslexia or parents of children with dyslexia, it does help to shift the stream of thought from disability to ability and this will stand children and adults with dyslexia in good stead (www. enable.org.uk).

Misconceptions

The misconceptions associated with dyslexia can cause some anxiety to parents and indeed to teachers. Although there is now an increasing awareness of dyslexia, there are still some misunderstandings shared by many regarding what exactly dyslexia is. Some see it as a reading disability while others, including many parents and teachers, see the wider implications of dyslexia, including memory and organisation as well as the social and emotional impact of dyslexia. The use and the 'misuse' of labels can also give rise to misunderstandings. Many arguments can be raised for and against the use of labels, but it is important that dyslexia is not covered up nor should the label be minimised or ignored.

The role of specialists

This book is focusing on school, college and university assessment – that is, teacher or specialist teacher assessment. These are the people who are in touch with the pupil or student, who know the learning context and how the individual responds to this and how he or she responds to different types of learning. But there is also scope and a need for specialist assessment.

There are a number of different professionals who can contribute to an assessment. It is useful to gather information from those who may have seen the child prior to the assessment. These professionals can of course complement teacher assessments. They can include:

- speech and language therapists
- medical professionals
- occupational therapists
- optometrists
- psychologists.

A description of the roles of these professionals is provided in Appendix 3 (page 137); however, the role of psychologists is discussed below, as they will most likely be the ones who will play a significant role in providing a diagnosis.

Psychologist

Woods (2016) suggests that in the UK the distinctive contribution of the psychologist has been frequently debated and can have many functions, such as consultation, assessment, intervention, research and training. This is clearly a very wide remit.

An early and groundbreaking working party report on dyslexia and psychological assessment (British Psychological Society, 1999) provided some insights into the roles of the psychologist in relation to dyslexia assessment. This has provided a framework for psychologists in the UK and has been used as a platform for their practice in schools and also in diagnosis.

In general, the main dilemmas for psychologists relate to 'testing' individual pupils as opposed to 'consulting' more broadly with schools.

In some countries such as the USA and Canada, and in countries in the Middle East, conducting psychometric and standardised assessments for dyslexia and other learning issues is the expectation, and the role of independent psychologists in private practice is both established and indeed welcomed.

What then can the psychologists do in relation to the dyslexia assessment? In our opinion as practising psychologists, the answer is a great deal. The psychologist is able to access closed tests. This includes the Wechsler Intelligence Scale for Children – WISC-V. Some of the other tests that can be used by a psychologist include those listed in Fig. 4.1 on the next page. Note that some of them can also be accessed by other professionals with appropriate qualifications. These are part of a battery of tests (and are not exclusive) that can be used in order to obtain useful information and a diagnosis of the nature and extent of the difficulty, as well as insights into the strengths.

The most useful psychometric tests are those that can provide diagnostic information as well as psychometric measures. Most tests can be interpreted diagnostically and it is important to look for information that can inform classroom practice as well as assist in a diagnosis.

Intelligence tests

There have been long-standing debates on the nature and use of intelligence tests for dyslexia, but the key point is that such tests should not be 'stand alone' items and the results in themselves need to be interpreted and applied to practice. It can be implied that if a student has low verbal IQ there will be clear implications for classroom practice. The data from intelligence tests can also contribute

Test	What it covers
Wechsler Intelligence Scale for Children (WISC-V)	Tests cognitive ability and intelligence as well as processing factors.
Wechsler Individual Achievement Test (WIAT-II and III)	Tests a range of achievement skills in literacy, numeracy and fluency.
Gray Oral Reading Tests (GORT- 5)	Tests reading fluency, rate, accuracy and comprehension.
Comprehensive Test of Phonological Processing (CTOPP-2)	Looks at phonological awareness, phonological memory and naming speed.
Wide Range Assessment of Memory and Learning (WRAML-2)	Focuses on a range of aspects of memory and learning including visual and verbal memory.
Test of Oral Language Development (TOLD-P4. and TOLD-I: 4)	Two versions: one for younger children and the other for children over eight years of age. Comprehensive test of different aspects of language including vocabulary, use of words and sentence development and sequencing. All the subtests are oral.
Test of Written Language (TOWL-4)	Provides a detailed assessment of written language – including spelling, writing conventions, expressive writing and structure.
Test of Orthographic Competence (TOC)	Comprehensive test on orthography – different types of spelling subtests are included as well as punctuation and several timed tests involving words.
Rapid Automatic Naming (RAN)	This test focuses on speed.

to a profile of the student's strengths and weaknesses and this can complement information from observation and from other standardised achievement tests.

The nature of the conventional IQ test means that some subtests are challenging for dyslexic individuals and that the aggregate score may not represent the individual's real intellectual ability, and for that reason it is important to see the aim of IQ testing as one that can reveal a profile that can be used to identify strengths and weaknesses and assist in the development of a teaching programme.

Miles also makes this point, arguing that dyslexics are 'strong on some tasks and relatively weak on others' (Miles, 1996, p. 177). Therefore, combining scores to produce a global IQ may mean that we underestimate the potential of the child or young person.

Barriers to learning

This should be seen within an assessment framework that highlights the barriers to learning experienced by the individual (see Fig. 4.2). This is important as it can also pinpoint the key intervention areas. It also underlines the point that assessment is not exclusively a test or testing process but needs to be broadened to incorporate aspects that may not be fully revealed in the testing process. It is therefore a good idea to develop a 'barriers to learning' framework, and the test results can confirm these factors and add to it.

Fig. 4.2: Potential barriers to learning: a framework to consider

Cognitive	Social/emotional	Environmental
Memory	Expectations	School ethos
Processing speed	Peer group comparison	Classroom layout
Sequencing	Self-esteem	School philosophy
Visual/auditory processing	Friendships	Space and scope for activities
Spatial awareness	Potential for success	Location of school in relation to home
Executive functioning	Participation in group activities	Student's work displayed
Reasoning and thinking skills	Home–school communication	Noise levels/access to technology

Summary

The key points covered in this chapter include the following:

1. Assessment does not provide the answer – it should provide questions that can be investigated and should help in the planning of learning.

2. It is important to consider assessment as a process that includes both formal and informal types of assessment.

3. When standardised tests are used, they should be selected carefully and appropriately, and a clear purpose and rationale should be obvious for selecting that particular test.

4. It is important that the process of data gathering is comprehensive and that this will include classroom teachers and parents and possibly referral to other professionals.

5. The psychologist can have a clear and distinct role in the assessment process in both testing and consultancy.

6. It is also important to refer to informal assessment through ongoing assessment and identifying the barriers to learning.

7. Above all assessment should link with intervention and should be seen as an ongoing process that can highlight the learner's strengths and weaknesses and support the learner in the development of their learning skills and capacities.

5 Assessment: understanding results and implications for practice

---

Chapter overview

This chapter will:

- provide some guidance in interpreting assessment results
- illustrate with reference to case studies the significance of some of the main findings from an assessment
- discuss the implications of assessment for teaching and learning.

As noted in the previous chapters, it is important to gather information from both informal and formal assessments. Informal relates to observation and diagnostic assessment as well as the performance of the student in different areas of the curriculum. Formal assessment tends to focus on standardised tests, including cognitive and achievement tests. This chapter will refer to both of these types of assessment. Classroom-based procedures for gathering information such as curriculum and subject assessment is discussed in Part 2.

Informal observation

The data from informal and observational assessments is usually quite straightforward, but this information in itself, although very helpful, will not provide sufficient evidence to warrant a diagnosis of dyslexia. Nevertheless, such information can reveal a great deal about the learner and the learner's preferences. Observing the student's learning preferences and how he or she deals with different areas of the curriculum, as well as his or her perception of his or her abilities, can be very helpful. Reid and Strnadová (2004) have developed a useful observation tool: Teacher Observation of Learning Styles (TOLS), which is provided in Appendix 4 and can be photocopied for classroom use (page 139). It includes key observation pointers for the teacher, which are organised into observation categories:

1. social – interaction and communication

2. environmental – mobility and time of day

3. emotional – persistence, responsibility and emotions

4. cognitive – modality preference, sequential or simultaneous learning

5. metacognitive – prediction, feedback and structure.

The information obtained from using TOLS can provide pointers to help understand the student's learning preferences and this can help identify the most appropriate teaching approaches.

Additionally it can help with classroom organisation, particularly when arranging students into groups for group work.

Reid and Strnadová (2004) also compiled a pupil/student inventory so that the learner can consider the style that is best for himself or herself: Pupil Assessment of Learning Style (PALS) (see Appendix 5, page 141). This is also divided into the same five broad categories: social, environmental, emotional, cognitive and metacognitive.

The responses from this type of informal observation assessment can have practical implications for the teacher and teaching. For example, learners with dyslexia are very often (although not always) visual/kinaesthetic learners and may also be global learners – meaning that they prefer to see the 'whole' before the 'individual pieces of information'. They may also prefer to work in groups and prefer discussion to reading.

One of the key questions that needs to be considered by the teacher when planning, following the use of this type of assessment inventory, is: 'how can I relate this to the learner, the task, the curriculum and the learning environment?' This is important and should be a prerequisite for developing curricular tasks.

Coffield (2004) argues that one needs to be careful about attempting to match teaching and learning style because of the conflicting research evidence. But the point remains that learning is more effective when the content and the context is familiar. This is very important for students with dyslexia. In addition to observation or a 'self-rating inventory', informal information can also be gathered through pre-task discussion. This can help to clarify the concepts and help to ensure that the pupils or student has an appropriate grasp of the concepts and an understanding of the background to the topic. Developing this with individuals with dyslexia is essential, as they need a framework and a structure to help with understanding and how to progress with the task. This can also pave the way for independent learning. It is important to present the information to the learner with dyslexia in a manner that is consistent with his or her preferences. Burden (2002) suggests that learning difficulties such as dyslexia may arise from difficulties at the 'input phase of information-processing'. This is because the learner may have an impulsive learning style. This means, according to Burden, that at the initial, vital stage of learning there is a breakdown in the learning process and this makes learning less efficient.

Formal assessment – linking assessment and intervention

As a prerequisite when using formal assessment, it is important to ensure that the test you choose is valid for your population of pupils or students and that it is well-standardised. It is important not to take this for granted.

Some of the factors to consider are:

- the size of the sample

- the age range of the sample

- the type of school in which the test was standardised – e.g. urban, rural, public sector, private sector

- the scoring system – e.g. does it give ages in years and months, age ranges or grade/year level?

- whether it provides percentiles and standard scores (see Glossary, page 149)

- how easy it is to interpret the scores

- whether there is comparison data with other similar tests available in the test manual

- whether the standardised tests have a high validity and reliability (see Glossary for an explanation of these, page 149) so that the teacher can use the data from the test with confidence.

Observation during testing

One of the issues with the popular trend of online testing is that it is difficult to judge the impact on the student of actually undertaking the test and of course the nature of the interaction with the assessor. Some of the important questions that can be answered through the tester and student interaction include:

- Is the student relaxed and calm?
- Does the student generate conversation or questions without being prompted?
- Is the student's voice confident or hesitant; loud or quiet, etc.?
- Is there any evidence of anxiety?
- Does the student's attitude or demeanor change with different types of tasks?
- Is there any sign of frustration?
- Is there evidence of any insecurities or competitiveness?

Responses from these points can help to provide information that can be useful.

Interpretation of results – linking with intervention

The results from tests are usually displayed in terms of standard scores and percentiles. These are important terms:

- **Standard score:** a standard score is one that has been transformed to fit a normal distribution curve. Usually it has a mean of 100 and a standard deviation of 15. This means that a student with a score of 85 would be one standard deviation below the mean.

- **Percentiles:** in percentiles the scores of students are arranged in rank order from lowest to highest. The lowest score is in the 1st percentile and the highest score is in the 99th percentile. Therefore if you scored in the 66th percentile, this would mean that you scored 'as well as or better than' 66% of the group. If your score was the same as 'the mean' for that test, then you scored in the 50th percentile.

Sometimes ages are used – but this is not as reliable a measure as standard scores. This is because there may be variations within the school system on what students are expected to do at certain ages.

Case study example

The following case study extract is based on a ten-year-old pupil assessed by a psychologist. The assessment aims to provide cognitive information as well as information on current attainments. The WISC-V was therefore used in addition to tests on reading, spelling and maths.

Fig. 5.1 on the next page shows the results from the cognitive assessment WISC-V. The key points that are indicated from the results are:

- The pupil is strong in the visual area in both visual spatial and fluid reasoning. Fluid reasoning involves the ability to solve novel 'on the spot' problems that cannot be performed by relying

Fig. 5.1: Wechsler Intelligence Scale for Children (WISC-V) test results for ten-year-old in case study

Indices	Composite score (mean=100)	Percentile rank	95% confidence interval	Qualitative description
Verbal comprehension	124	95	114–130	High
Visual spatial	135	99	125–140	Very high
Fluid reasoning	126	96	117–131	High
Working memory	82	12	76–91	Below average
Processing speed	89	23		Low average
Full scale IQ	119	90	113–124	Above average
General ability index (this discounts processing speed and working memory)	132	98	124–137	Very high
Cognitive proficiency (this includes processing speed and working memory)	81	10	75–90	Below average

exclusively on previously learned habits or schemas. In the WISC-V this involves a visual reasoning test using pictures.

- The pupil has excellent verbal comprehension skills and an excellent vocabulary.

- Overall the pupil's language scores are in the high range.

- The reasoning scores – that is, language and visual reasoning – are at a very high level. These scores comprise what is known as the 'general ability index' (GAI) and in this case the score is in the high range. This therefore indicates that the pupil has a great deal of ability and potential.

- On the weaker side it can be seen that the working memory score is weak and in the lower 12th percentile compared to verbal comprehension, which is in the 95th percentile.

- It should be noted that apart from processing speed all the subtests in the WISC-V are oral.

- It can also be noted that the processing speed score is weak and on the low side of average. Again this contrasts with the high verbal and visual scores.

- This is a student with a high understanding of language who is able to solve new problems. The low working memory score may restrict the student as this will mean that he will have difficulty processing information in the short term and carrying out two or more activities at the same time. This can have an impact on a range of classroom activities and would likely mean that instructions would need to be repeated.

- It can be noted that this student is also low in processing speed and this can have implications for written work and for keeping up with the work of the class. It is likely that the student would need more time in exams and in class. This can also have implications for homework.

- The cognitive proficiency provides an indication of the processing scores – that is, working memory and processing speed. Pupils with dyslexia would usually be higher in the reasoning side compared to the processing.

Fig. 5.2: Wechsler Individual Achievement Test (WIAT-III) – test results for ten-year-old in case study

Dimension	Subtests	Standard score	Percentile rank	Qualitative description
Listening comprehension	Receptive vocabulary*	120	91	Above average
Maths	Maths problem-solving	110	75	Average
	Numerical operations	88	23	Low average
	Maths fluency	112	79	High average
Reading	Word reading	88	23	Low average
	Pseudo-word decoding	84	16	Below average
Spelling	Single-word spelling	84	16	Below average
Oral expression	Expressive vocabulary*	123	94	High
Essay composition	Word count	84	16	Below average
	Text organisation	84	16	Below Average
	Grammar	84	16	Below Average

*These are visual subtests using picture cues

Once these results have been obtained, it is then important to look at the results of the attainment tests for reading, spelling and writing as well as numeracy.

The WIAT–III is a very comprehensive test and this can be seen in the results of the case study for the ten-year-old in Fig. 5.2 above. The results of the test show the following:

Reading

The student is low in reading single words and his decoding is in the low average range. In this case decoding refers to pseudo-word reading, which is nonsense words, and this is seen as a valid test of decoding. The results would indicate that he has difficulties in word attack skills and also a difficulty in reading words by sight. It is likely therefore that this, student will have difficulty with reading fluency (speed) and possibly reading comprehension. In order to check this, the Gray Oral Reading Tests were used as they look at accuracy, fluency and reading comprehension. The results of these tests are shown below:

Fig. 5.3: Gray Oral Reading Tests (GORT–5) – test results for ten-year-old in case study

Subtest	Standard score	Percentile rank	Qualitative description
Reading comprehension	89	23	Low average
Reading fluency	84	16	Below average
Reading accuracy	88	23	Low average
Reading rate	84	16	Below average

It can be seen that the student is low in all the reading areas. If we were to look at his predicted level using the cognitive test as a measure, it would be seen that he should be reading well above his reading age. These scores indicate that he is reading lower that his chronological age and well below his predicted level of reading.

Comment

A combination of these factors – that is, his cognitive weaknesses (working memory and processing speed), high oral language comprehension skills, low reading speed, accuracy and comprehension and low word attack skills – would indicate dyslexia.

Dyslexia is often seen as a difficulty in phonological processing, and to confirm the diagnosis, the Comprehensive Test of Phonological Processing (CTOPP) was used. The result is shown below in Fig. 5.4. The figure shows the results of the indices, which combine a number of related subtests.

Fig. 5.4: Comprehensive Test of Phonological Awareness (CTOPP) – test results for ten-year-old in case study

Subtest	Standard score	Percentile	Category
Phonological awareness	85	16	Low average
Memory for digits	84	16	Below average
Rapid letter naming	80	9	Below average

From this, it can be seen that:

- the student has difficulties in phonological awareness as well as working memory and speed – this is an oral speed test that is different from the previous one shown in the WISC-V
- the overall results in reading and sub-skills of reading strongly suggest that the student has dyslexia.

It should be noted that there is no evidence of sensory impairment, e.g. visual or hearing difficulties, but it is a good idea to ask the parents or carers to check this prior to the assessment, as noted in Chapter 4 (page 39).

Additionally the student's main language is English – EAL children may also show reading issues, but it is unlikely that their verbal comprehension would be as high. The issues relating to English as an additional language are discussed in Chapter 10.

Other factors: spelling

It can be noted that the student is also low in spelling. This is also unexpected in relation to his abilities. This is important information but in order to provide guidance for classroom practice, it is necessary to analyse his spelling errors and the spelling pattern. For example, are letters missing, which may indicate some visual problems? For example, in the word 'rhythm' the 'y' or the first 'h' may be missing.

Word confusion can also account for spelling errors and this means the student needs to have a context for spelling but also has to overlearn the use of that word. An example can be seen in the words 'sight' and 'cite'. This type of error can be assessed in the Test of Orthographic Competence (TOC). An example of the results of this test is shown in Fig. 5.5.

Fig. 5.5: The Test of Orthographic Competence (TOC) – test results for ten-year-old pupil

Subtest	Standard score	Percentile	Category
Sight spelling	84	16	Below average
Word scramble*	90	25	Average
Letter choice *	92	27	Average
Punctuation	95	37	Average
Homophone choice	84	16	Below average

*timed test

In this test the subtest 'homophone choice' is a good indication of the use of the wrong word. For example, the spellings of a word that has two spellings and meanings are shown – 'meat' and 'meet' – and this is accompanied by a picture of the correct item, and the student has to indicate which of the two words represent the spelling of the word shown in the picture. A low score in this subtest can have implications for practice in relation to developing written vocabulary. Indeed, this type of error can usually be readily noted in the written work of a pupil with dyslexia. This test has a different version for pupils aged eight to 12 (above) and aged 13+. In the 13+ test, the homophone choice test is called 'word choice' and three different spellings of the same word are shown but only one is correct. The student has to select the correct one. Visual skills are important for this type of subtest.

The 'sight' spelling subtest in the TOC is also a good indication of the type of spelling errors. In this subtest, part of the word is provided and the student has to fill in the blanks. This means they are relying on how the word looks visually.

In misspellings, the use of incorrect vowels is quite common, e.g. the word 'dependent' is often spelt as 'dependant' and the word 'separate' spelt as 'seperate'. This can indicate some auditory issues and difficulty with pronunciation. In relation to pronunciation, misspellings with voiced and unvoiced words can also be seen. An example of this would be 'd' and 't' – both involve the same vocal chord and tongue mechanism but the sound made is different, as in the word 'boy', which has a voiced sound at the beginning of the word, compared to the word 'toy', which has an unvoiced beginning sound.

Reversals of the letter order are also quite common with pupils and students with dyslexia, particularly with double vowels, e.g. in the words 'niece' and 'pharaoh', which can be spelt 'neice 'and 'pharoah'.

Poor phonological awareness can also account for spelling difficulties. For example, the child may omit one of the sounds in the word. In a study analysing spelling errors of children with dyslexia, Protopapas et al. (2013) noted that dyslexic children differed from non-dyslexic children by making more errors of the same type, in comparable relative proportions. If the errors are categorised by poor phonological representations then this clearly provides a path for intervention.

It is important to obtain a spelling score in an expressive writing piece as opposed to a single-words test, which may have been previously learnt.

Other factors: writing

It is important to take other factors into account when interpreting the results of the assessment. This includes handwriting, writing speed and the quality of expressive writing. These are discussed below.

Handwriting

It is important to note the quality and consistency of the letter formation and overall handwriting style. In pupils who have a severe and enduring handwriting difficulty it is possible to diagnose dysgraphia (see Chapter 8, page 106 and Glossary, page 149). Some of the points to consider include:

- hand dominance
- pencil grip
- posture
- paper position
- pressure on paper
- wrist movement
- letter formation
- left to right orientation
- reversals of letters
- spacing
- letter size and formation consistency
- style – joins in letters
- speed
- fatigue factors.

These factors can have an impact on the individual's performance and self-esteem and this is also evident in some pupils and students with dyslexia.

Some suggestions to deal with this include the following:

- Consider alternatives to hand-written responses, such as the use of a laptop or tablet.
- It is important not to penalise the student for poor presentation of work or for mis-spellings.
- Provide some guidelines for writing, particularly on the use of paragraph headings. A structure for extended writing is important and software such as *Inspiration*™ can help with this.
- Ensure the student receives rest periods when extended writing is required.

Expressive writing

This is a more prevalent difficulty experienced by pupils and students with dyslexia. This can be seen in the case study extract in this chapter. The student's written work was low for word count, text organisation and grammar. It is also important to look at the content of the written work, and the Test of Written Language (TOWL) does this. It looks at the composition and structure of written work as well as the content and spelling. This is a comprehensive test and one that can yield a great deal of relevant information, which can not only assist in the diagnosis of dyslexia, but also inform teaching.

Often the results show that the student needs support with organisation of written work. It is therefore essential that the student is provided with a structure to help with writing. Students with dyslexia will often need support with a number of aspects of writing. These include:

- **Organisation –** making logical connections.
- **Planning –** the importance of planning cannot be underplayed and students with dyslexia can have significant difficulties with this. This can be particularly frustrating for students.

- **Sequencing** – the content needs to be in an appropriate sequence and this is a very common difficulty for students with dyslexia. They can practise by indicating the sequence orally before beginning to write.
- **Identifying key points** – it is important that the written piece has all the relevant points. This is also a common problem for students with dyslexia and they can insert information that is not totally relevant to the topic.
- **Imagination** – usually students with dyslexia will have a good imagination but they may need support to harness this into a written form.
- **Starting and finishing** – these are important aspects of writing and it is important that the student obtains practice at writing opening paragraphs and summing up for a conclusion.

Analysing the student's written work can be revealing and can point towards intervention. It should be noted that many students with dyslexia would have difficulty performing at the same level in written work as they do orally. This type of discrepancy is well worth noting.

Other factors: numeracy

Although numeracy is different from the factors discussed above, maths and number work are very much processing activities. The individual with dyslexia may therefore have difficulties with the processing activities in numeracy, but perhaps will be able to understand the concepts. Lack of confidence can also be a factor in maths difficulties for students with dyslexia. This can be highlighted in the WIAT-III table shown earlier in the numerical operations test, which involves practical number work – a processing activity – and maths reasoning, which involves 'understanding' (although there is also some processing connected to this too).

Feedback

After any assessment, it is important to provide some feedback to the student as well as to parents and teachers. Clearly the type and extent of the feedback depends on the age of the student, but students of all ages need some form of feedback.

Feedback to younger pupils

In younger pupils, it is important to tell them what they did well – even if it is just completing the test or part of the test. But find a point that can be praised and give the pupil positive encouragement.

Feedback to older students

It is also important to provide positive points when giving feedback to older students, and always start with complimentary comments.

You can ask them what they found most difficult and what was more straightforward. You can then give them some idea of the results, indicating the areas they found challenging and how this can be dealt with. The idea of the feedback should be to give them confidence to work on those challenging areas.

Feedback should be as specific as possible and relate to the student's strengths as well as their challenges. It can also help the student identify new goals and help them develop enhanced self-knowledge in their own learning.

Feedback to teachers and parents

This should include the following:

- Details of the tests administered and the reasons why particular tests were used.
- The child's test behaviour and motivation – was he or she interested in the test materials? Did the student manage to maintain interest throughout the assessment?
- The results – how do they compare to the norm (average)?
- The implications of the results – this is important as the results should provide information on a diagnosis and, importantly, recommendations for intervention or further assessment.
- Follow-up assessment and details of any monitoring of progress that will be carried out. This is also important, and arrangements and a time sequence for monitoring of progress should be indicated. It is important to reassure parents and teachers that the assessment is not the end of the process – in many cases it is the beginning.
- Details of short-, medium- and long-term monitoring should be indicated, although this can best be negotiated with the school.

Implications for practice

It is important to indicate that the assessment will not necessarily provide a ready-made programme, but rather suggestions for practice (Wolf and Reid, 2015). Teachers themselves will have ideas on how to progress and it is important to ensure that, as far as possible, the teacher is involved in the assessment process. The notion of a reflective practitioner is important. Schön (1987) suggests that reflective practitioners notice what is different or unusual about patterns of progress in student learning. They think carefully and deeply about what assessment information is telling them about the student and can readjust their own understanding of the student based on this and also their own teaching.

Implications for intervention

It is a good idea to highlight the key areas for intervention by referring to the implications of the results of the assessment – that includes both informal and formal assessment. Fig. 5.6 highlights what the implications of the results might be and suggests areas for intervention.

Fig. 5.6: Intervention table

Area of difficulty	Implications	Intervention/resources
Reading fluency	The student will take a long time to read and this can be very discouraging. Additionally it can have an impact on reading comprehension as there is a relationship between reading fluency and reading comprehension.	Try high–low books that are high in interest and low in vocabulary. These can help with fluency (e.g. books by Barrington Stoke). Help the student to read using skimming and scanning strategies. This means that the key words are highlighted and the student will be able to read quicker than if every word is read. Students with dyslexia often stick at small words such as 'but' and 'before' so cutting out these words can help reading speed.

Fig. 5.6: Continued

Area of difficulty	Implications	Intervention/resources
Reading accuracy	The student will be discouraged from reading and the text may not make much sense as some of the difficult words will be omitted or read incorrectly.	Many strategies can be used for this depending on the reason for the difficulties with accuracy. If the problem is decoding or phonics, then word attack skills will be needed. A multisensory programme such as Units of Sound (Dyslexia Action Training) or Orton Gillingham (OG) – Canada and USA is advised for decoding difficulties. The Rose Report (2009) recommends a synthetics phonics programme, and programmes like *Jolly Phonics* and *Nessy* can help with this. If the problem is a visual one then Crossbow Education (www.crossboweducation.co.uk) have a large number of materials that can help with this. It may also be due to a lack of sight words and in this case reading experience can be suggested. Paired reading is a good example of this.
Reading comprehension	Reading will not be very interesting for the student and will feel very much like an ordeal or chore.	It is a good idea to ensure that the student reads only small pieces of text and is given more time to reread for comprehension. Pre-reading discussion can help with this as some of the key words can be highlighted. The student will be able to develop a schema or framework for the passage and this will help with comprehension. Most reading schemes and programmes will have exercises on comprehension. It is also important to encourage the student to self-question for comprehension.
Difficulty with inferential reading	This means the reader will take the passage literally and have difficulty in reading between the lines. This can be a common problem for students with dyslexia.	The student needs to be encouraged to use strategies and questions that can help with inferential reading. This can include questions such as: • What do you think will happen next? • Why do you think she said what she did? • How do you think…? • What kind of person was _____? • Why did _____ happen?
Difficulty with the concepts and reflecting on what has been read for deeper meaning	This can result in the student not acquiring higher-order thinking skills and it may mean that his/her understanding of the passage is at a basic level.	Some suggestions for dealing with this involve encouraging the learner to ask questions in order to obtain some clarification and understanding at a deeper level. This can involve the following cycle: Questioning – 'Why, what, where, how?' Clarifying – 'I see, but what about this?' Understanding – 'Right, I get it now!' Connecting – 'I did something like this last week.' Directing – 'Okay, I know what to do now.' Monitoring – 'Maybe I should do this now – that does not seem to be correct.' Assessing – 'So far, so good'; 'I think I am on the right track.'

Fig. 5.6: Continued

Area of difficulty	Implications	Intervention/resources
Spelling	Can result in the student being reluctant to write.	For younger pupils, try 'simultaneous oral spelling'. The steps for this include: • having the word written correctly, or made with the letter • saying the word • writing the word, spelling out each letter as it is written, using cursive script. The student needs to see each letter, hear its name and receive kinaesthetic feedback through the movement of the arm and throat muscles. Check to see if the word is correct. Cover up the word and repeat the process. Continue to practise the word in this way, three times a day, for one week. By this time the word should be committed to memory. However, only one word will have been learned. This final step involves the categorisation of the word with other words that sound and look alike. So if the word that has been learned is 'round', the student is then shown that he can also spell 'ground', 'pound', 'found', 'mound', 'sound', 'around', 'bound', 'grounded', 'pounding', etc. Therefore, six, eight or more words have been learnt for the effort of one.
Expressive writing	The student can become easily discouraged, which can also have an impact on self-esteem.	Provide the student with a list of key words that can be used in a piece of writing. These words can be divided into different categories such as: descriptive words, names, places, 'feeling' words. The use of cloze passages (a passage with some words missing) can be a good exercise and the student can fill in the blanks from a list that is provided. Help the student create a personal word bank. It is a good idea to have the meaning of the word next to the word to ensure that the student uses the word appropriately. The use of an electronic talking dictionary (e.g. www.franklin.com) can also be useful.

Summary

This chapter has highlighted a range of assessment materials that can be used in a dyslexia assessment. Not all the tests described in this chapter need to be used and there are others that can be used instead (see Online Resources). It is important that each assessment for dyslexia is treated individually. Although there will be similarities in profile and in the presenting difficulties, it is still important to gather the pre-assessment background and decide on an assessment strategy. As indicated in this chapter, assessment should be seen as a process and this can include more than a test.

It is important that assessment should link to, and inform, practice. Feedback to parents and other members of staff is also important, particularly if accommodations are to be made. It is also important that time is taken and appropriate feedback is provided to the student – an assessment can be an anxious time for an individual and he or she may not show this.

These points are highlighted in the following two chapters, which focus on the curriculum and how dyslexia can be identified within everyday class work.

PART 2

Curriculum assessment

6 Assessment through differentiation

Chapter overview

This chapter will:

- look at the role of differentiation in assessment
- consider different types of differentiation and their implications for assessment and intervention
- look at the role of self-assessment
- discuss differentiation in different subject areas of the curriculum
- provide an observational framework that can be used with differentiation.

Assessment through differentiation is an example of informal assessment. The benefit of this type of assessment is that it does not compare the student's performance against others in the class, but rather against him- or herself. In other words it looks at the individual's own personal progress, and any progress can be noted and monitored. This is very useful for recording the particular areas the student has made progress in and those that still remain stagnant. This will inform planning and intervention. It is important to link assessment, planning and intervention.

What do we mean by differentiation for learners with dyslexia?

Differentiation is the vehicle by which teachers can help learners with dyslexia access the full curriculum. This can be achieved in four ways:

1. differentiation by task (includes content and presentation)
2. differentiation by outcome (results)
3. differentiation by resources (materials)
4. differentiation by support (intervention).

All of these are discussed below.

Identifying barriers to learning through differentiation

Almost any type of potential or actual barrier or difficulty can be identified through differentiation. This can apply to all aspects of reading and writing as well as processing speed (responding to tasks) and memory (recall and recognition), and presentation (grammar, structure and organisation) of written work. Additionally, information on motivation and social and emotional issues can also be identified from observing and using differentiation as an assessment tool (see Fig. 6.1, next page).

Fig. 6.1: Potential role of informal assessment using differentiated methods and how this can link with intervention

Skill to be measured	What to look for	Evidence	Possible intervention
Reading speed	Fluency and reading rate – taking accuracy into account for fluency.	Timed passages – formal or informal timing.	Timed games and fun activities. Accommodations such as extra time.
Reading accuracy	Pattern of errors in reading aloud.	Missing out words or lines. Hesitations. Lack of whole-word reading. Lack of reading punctuation.	Phonic programme if there is a decoding difficulty. Paired reading or shared reading if there is difficulty with accuracy and fluency.
Reading comprehension	Lack of understanding of passage. Lack of understanding of specific vocabulary.	Cannot summarise passage. Does not have the general idea of the passage. Cannot answer specific questions.	Reciprocal reading – i.e. shared reading and question and answer tasks after reading.
Spelling	Pattern of spelling errors.	Inappropriate use of double consonants, e.g. 'rr' or 'tt' in 'parrot'. Difficulty with spelling rules.	Spelling software programmes or support such as *Texthelp*. Support methods such as 'look, say, write and check'. Simultaneous oral spelling.
Handwriting	Inconsistency in style and direction of strokes. Illegibility, spacing and inappropriate use of capitals.	Give timed and untimed handwriting tests and note the differences. Note the points in the previous column.	Consider alternatives to handwriting. Allow rest periods when extended writing is required. Provide blank copies of diagrams and charts, indicating where responses should be inserted.
Expressive writing	Length and quality of written piece. Relevance of written work, structure and grammar.	Make a note of the previous points and ensure you time the written piece. Try both conditions: timed and untimed.	It is important to provide a structure for all written tasks. Encourage the use of a laptop. Provide small steps for written work.
Number work and maths	Time taken to complete a maths question. Understanding of a task. Accuracy with rote calculations.	Clarity of working – spot where the mistakes were made. Overreliance on calculator.	Calculator or formulae supplied. Use of maths websites (e.g. www.mathsexplained.co.uk). Use of visual strategies to remember formulae, e.g. to help visualise the difference between > 'is greater than' and < 'is less than' – show signs as open mouths waiting to devour the largest number.

Fig. 6.1: Continued

Skill to be measured	What to look for	Evidence	Possible intervention
Attention issues	Length and number of time spent off-task. Easily distracted.	Incomplete work.	Look at classroom environment and make modifications to help, e.g. dim lights; seat at front; clear desk; structured tasks.
Emotional issues and anxiety	Does the learner show any signs of stress? Can the student be left to work independently? Can the student persist with the task or will he or she require monitoring? Can the learner only work for short periods? Does the learner require constant reassurance? Is the learner aware of the needs of others?	Avoidance of work. Uncharacteristic behaviours for the student, such as hiding work or copying. Completing work too quickly. Asks lots of questions repeatedly. May not fit into a class group.	Discussion with parents. Structure work and monitor frequently. Differentiate the task so that he or she can complete it. Provide a brain break and then suggest additional points. Provide clear and extended written instructions and go over these with the learner. Select a buddy from the class for the child to work with.

Essentially, effective differentiation should overcome the learning barriers, and the differentiated materials produced should aim to minimise these barriers. At the same time, it is important to obtain the evidence of the student's specific learning issues as this can point to more effective and perhaps more specific intervention.

An explanation of the different types of differentiation is shown below, together with an indication of the implications for assessment.

Differentiation by task (content and presentation)

Content

Differentiation by task involves the process of adapting materials to suit a range of learner's abilities and level of attainments.

How this can be achieved will depend on the student's individual learning needs so it is important that an informal assessment takes place prior to differentiating the task. Some suggestions include:

- **Abridged books:** These are books that have been condensed or shortened. The language is simplified and some of the information that could be considered unnecessary is taken out. In a non-fiction text, the abridged version would summarise the main points as briefly as possible.

- **Abridged workbooks:** These are often available to accompany a novel study. It is important to ensure the workbooks are still challenging to the individual student.

- **Audio books:** Abridgement can also be a book that has been adapted into an audio version to use as a companion with the original version. Audio books are often available in both an abridged version and an unabridged version. The unabridged version is good if a student has poor reading skills but wants to follow along with the text or wants to appreciate the book in its entirety. This can be extremely beneficial in helping to develop the student's language experience and extending their vocabulary as well as providing an insight into narrative and story plots. The abridged version is good for simply following the storyline and will of course be much quicker to finish.

Presentation of material

Differentiation by task also includes how the material is presented. For example:

- **Font** – retype in a larger, more dyslexic-friendly font such as Century Gothic; this can make it easier for students to read.
- **Paper** – use a different-coloured paper or different-coloured font. Some students are distracted by the glare off white paper.
- **Key points** – provide a list of key points using bullets.
- **Heading and subheadings** – the organisational structure can make it much easier for a dyslexic student to read and understand.
- **Visual aids** – e.g. mind maps, spider grams, graphic organisers.
- **Key words or phrases** – these can be highlighted for the student.
- **Quantity** – provide the student with smaller amounts of information by breaking information down.

Implications for assessment

The assessment should give some indication regarding how the material should be presented and how to make the task or content accessible to the learner, e.g. it may be necessary to:

- reword the directions or instructions with simple vocabulary and clear, short sentences in a logical, sequential order, or keep the concept and ideas the same but change the vocabulary to be more easily understood
- read instructions one step at a time to the student
- adapt the task to fit the strengths of the student
- graduate the task from simple to more complex
- vary the activities or learning strategies to give the student alternatives to explore the content, e.g. they may use graphs or webs to show their comprehension of the concepts rather than writing a paragraph
- focus on the content of their writing rather than the spelling, punctuation and grammar
- allow a student to use a picture dictionary where or when it is appropriate.

It may also be useful to reassess after differentiated materials have been used. This can involve further planning as in the 'assess, plan, do, review' model as outlined in the SEND Code of Practice in England (DfE and Department of Health, 2015) and discussed in Chapter 2 (page 25).

The assessment should also suggest the use of multisensory teaching, e.g.:

- Use all the learning pathways in the brain: visual, auditory, tactile, kinaesthetic.
- Ensure the tasks involve active learning, e.g. tracking while reading, asking questions during reading passages, tracing over letters or words.

- Change positions; try sitting on a ball, standing on a balance board, writing on a whiteboard, lying on the floor, reading in beanbag chairs or on cushions on the floor.
- Play games to reinforce concepts (e.g. see Crossbow Education for a range of phonic games: www.crossboweducation.com/phonic%20games.htm).

Differentiation by outcome (results)

Implications for assessment

The following could be considered within the assessment process:

- **Opportunities to talk and discuss in the classroom:** This can allow students to engage in 'print-free' debate and utilise their strengths in oral discussion. Talking through an issue can help students develop logical thinking skills and reflect and elaborate on their understanding. Additionally, practice in discussion can also have an impact on the student's ability to question, infer, deduce, propose and evaluate.
- **Make the assessment more appropriate and effective:** Differentiation is not only about making classwork and the printed material more accessible for students with dyslexia, but it is also about making the assessment more appropriate and effective. It can be argued that traditional forms of assessment can disadvantage the dyslexic student because usually there is a discrepancy (and this may be a significant discrepancy) between their understanding of a topic and how they are able to display that understanding in written form. This may be overcome through continuous and portfolio assessment in most subject areas.
- **Encourage self-assessment:** One of the aims of differentiation is to provide structured support to the learner to help him or her acquire self-sufficiency in learning. A key component of this is the ability to be able to assess one's own performance. The learner therefore needs to be encouraged to monitor his or her own performance and to ask the right type of questions that can lead to self-assessment. Differentiation is the ideal vehicle to achieve this – for example, some self-questions that can help with self-monitoring and lead to self-assessment.

Strategies to develop understanding of text

- **Questioning:** It is essential that students have the opportunity to interact and engage with texts and move beyond literal comprehension. They need to consider questions that require them to deduce, infer, justify and evaluate, and this can lead to self-assessment.
- **Literal questions:** Repeating directly, or in their own words, what the text says, e.g. Can you tell me what happened when/where/who? What are the main points in this non-fiction text? This can form the foundation for developing self-monitoring, as the basic facts have to be known.
- **Inferential questions:** Reading between the lines, drawing out conclusions that are based on, but go beyond, the information given in the text. This is the crucial area and one that the student needs to acquire if he or she is to develop self-assessment.
- **Deductive questions:** Drawing conclusions from the information given throughout the text, e.g. Explain X using two or more points to justify this. Where does it imply that? This can lead to higher-order thinking skills.
- **Justification:** Finding evidence in the text to justify responses, e.g. What in the text makes you say that? This, along with the next point (evaluative questions), holds the key to competent

self-assessment. If the student can display justification and evaluation then it is likely they have understood and can monitor and assess their competence in that area.

- **Evaluative questions:** Making critical judgements relating to the text, e.g. Is this a successful piece of persuasive writing? What makes you think that? Does this passage succeed in creating suspense? Why/How?

These points are extremely important for students with dyslexia, as it is too easy for them just to complete the task at a level well below their capabilities. It is important that they are encouraged to engage in higher-order thinking skills, and self-assessment and differentiation can be vehicles to develop these skills.

Differentiation by resources (materials)

Resources can be important for differentiation but they should be seen as complementary. It needs to be appreciated that differentiation is a broad concept and includes more than accessing a range of materials and resources. Resources can support differentiation and should be seen as an add-on and not the mainstay of differentiation.

Implications for assessment

It is important to select the most appropriate resources and that is why a detailed formal and informal assessment is necessary. For example, if the reading problem is decoding, you have to decide whether it is because the student does not have the basic phonological knowledge of words or has visual issues, which means he or she misreads letters and words. Additionally the problem may be due to poor phonological or visual memory. In that case, memory game resources should be obtained (e.g. from Crossbow Education, see Glossary and Resources, pages 149 and 151). If the resources are appropriate for the student, then the assessment outcome can be quite different. This provides a good rationale for linking assessment with intervention.

Differentiation by support (intervention)

It needs to be acknowledged that some students with dyslexia will need a teaching assistant (TA) or some other form of additional support. The range of duties and responsibilities for TAs varies considerably from school to school. Some have considerable responsibility and are involved in planning and assessment as well as in the teaching and learning process. Others may have little or no responsibility and carry out prescribed tasks only.

Irrespective of their role, TAs are in a key position to form a close interaction with students and to obtain a good understanding of an individual's needs. Since some students with dyslexia will have access to TAs, it is important that TAs are familiar with dyslexia and have an understanding of the needs of young people with dyslexia. There will be training implications here and it is crucial that all members of staff are included in school professional development courses. For example, a TA can monitor a student's progress and also encourage that individual to begin to monitor his or her own work and eventually self-assess. TAs are in a good position to carry out this type of activity and, overall, this form of ongoing assessment is very valuable as it is a good example of linking assessment with teaching.

The role of differentiation in informing the development of a learning plan

Some other factors that can be associated with differentiation and can inform the development of a learning plan are:

- **Knowledge of the student's strengths and difficulties:** This is essential, especially since not all students with dyslexia will display the same profile. This is therefore the best starting point, as often strengths can be utilised to help deal with the weaknesses. For example, students with dyslexia often have a preference for visual and kinaesthetic learning (experiential learning) and a difficulty with auditory learning. Phonics, which relies heavily on sounds and therefore the auditory modality, needs to be introduced together with visual and experiential forms of learning. The tactile modality involving touch and feeling the shape of letters that make specific sounds should also be utilised, as well as the visual symbol of these letters and letter/sound combinations. Similarly many of the questions in standardised tests are administered orally and this can prove to be disadvantageous for students with dyslexia. It is not uncommon for students with dyslexia to underperform in standardised tests.

- **Consultation to inform assessment:** The responsibility for dealing with students with dyslexia within the classroom should not solely rest with the class teacher. Ideally it should be seen as a 'whole-school' responsibility. This means that consultation with school management and other colleagues is important, and equally it is important that time is allocated for this. Information from previous teachers, support staff, school management and parents are all important and such joint liaison can help to ensure the necessary collaboration to provide support for the class teacher. Importantly, this should be built into the school procedures and not be a reaction to a problem that has occurred – such collaboration can therefore be seen as preventative and proactive and can inform assessment at an early stage in the process.

- **Current level of literacy acquisition:** An accurate and full assessment of the student's current levels of attainment is necessary in order to effectively plan a programme of learning. The assessment should include listening comprehension as well as reading accuracy and fluency. Listening comprehension can often be a more accurate guide to the abilities and understanding of dyslexic students than reading and spelling accuracy. Indeed, it is often the discrepancy between listening comprehension and reading accuracy that can be a key factor in identifying dyslexia. Information on the levels of attainment will be an instrumental factor in planning for differentiation.

- **Cultural factors:** Background knowledge, particularly cultural factors, is important, as this can influence the selection of books and whether some of the concepts in the text need to be singled out for additional and differentiated explanation. Cultural values are an important factor. It has been suggested that the 'big dip' in performance noted in some bilingual pupils in later primary school may be explained by a failure of professionals to understand and appreciate the cultural values and the actual level of competence of the bilingual pupil, particularly in relation to conceptual development and competence in thinking skills. It is possible for teachers to misinterpret bilingual pupils' development of good phonic skills in the early stages of literacy development in English, and they may in fact fail to note the difficulties that these pupils might be having with comprehension. When the difficulties later emerge, these pupils can be grouped inappropriately with native speakers of English who have the more conventional problems with phonic awareness, or their difficulties are assumed to derive from specific perceptual problems rather than from the cultural unfamiliarity of the text. In order for a teaching approach with bilingual students to be fully effective it has to be comprehensive, which means that it needs to incorporate the views of parents and the community. This requires considerable preparation and pre-planning, as well as consultation with parents and community organisations.

Subject differentiation examples: mathematics, music and physical education

Clearly, subject differentiation needs to be implemented across the whole curriculum, although three examples from different subject areas are selected here to highlight some key points.

Mathematics: barriers to learning

Abstract concepts and ideas can be difficult for students with dyslexia as they require organisation and access to knowledge, rules, techniques, skills and concepts. Rules that play an important part in mathematics have often to be rote-learned. Other skills that may be difficult to access for students with dyslexia are the spatial skills that are needed to help understand shape, symmetry, size and quantity and linear skills that are needed to help understand sequence, order and the representations found in the number system. These aspects can prove demanding for dyslexic students, and in addition they still have the literacy challenges and other cognitive difficulties associated with dyslexia, such as working memory, speed of processing and automaticity. These can all have implications for mathematics and for assessing difficulties in mathematics. For example, students with dyslexia may not understand the meaning of words such as 'difference', 'evaluate', 'odd', 'mean' and 'product' in the context of mathematics.

The following factors can also contribute to the demands of mathematics for students with dyslexia:

- **Linear and sequential processing** – this can be demanding because dyslexic students usually have some difficulty with order and sequencing and these are crucial in order to obtain the correct response in some mathematics problems.

- **Precision** – this is also necessary and one slip up in the processing of a problem can result in a wrong answer, even though the student may have a good understanding of the problem and the process.

- **Accuracy and detail** – because individuals with dyslexia tend to be more global and random in their thinking.

- **Long-term memory and information retrieval** – these can be problematic for students with dyslexia.

- **Lack of organisation at the cognitive level** – that is, at the initial stage of learning; if learning is not organised at this crucial initial stage then retrieval will be difficult at a later stage.

- **Effective storage of information** – students with dyslexia may have some difficulty with effective storage as well as accessing and retrieving information. It is for that reason that learning styles in mathematics are important; assisting a student in utilising a preferred learning style can help effective storage, retrieval and access to information.

- **Working memory** – this can also present some difficulties because working memory implies that students need to hold information in their short-term store, which could be a fraction of a second, and process that information into meaningful stimuli. This is very important in mathematics as mental operations are necessary to do this, which can be demanding for students with dyslexia.

Support strategies for mathematics and dyslexia

The strategies below can be used in informal assessment and they can also help to identify the student's learning preferences and the mode of learning he or she is most comfortable with. This can link assessment with intervention.

- Always write down the working out of a problem so the student can retrace their steps if necessary, and keep the template within view of the student.
- Make the teaching multi-sensory with the use of age-appropriate concrete materials. Older students will use playing cards, dominoes and darts.
- Use the links to other subjects, e.g. grids in geography, or measurement in graphics and science.
- Use visual devices to help children remember formulae – get them to visualise, for example, the > 'is greater than' and the < 'is less than' signs as open mouths waiting to devour the largest number.
- Mind-map the terms and phrases that we use when we want to perform the operation called subtraction: minus; take away; how many fewer; how many less. Remember that sometimes we have to do the opposite operation to the way the language appears to be heading us.
- Plan backwards – write down the most difficult thing that you want students to know by the end of a unit and break it down into smaller skills, e.g. to be able to do this, you must be able to do this. An example might be angles. To understand angles, you need to know number facts to 90, 180 and 360, so you would start your unit with the most basic skill of addition/subtraction.
- Use maths puzzles – have a puzzle of the week, and get the students to find puzzles to challenge the class.

Music: barriers to learning

The following are barriers to learning that music can present for students with dyslexia:

- **Relates to learning a new language:** Students have to learn the meaning of symbols, some with only subtle differences between them, and know when and how to use them.
- **Requires visual and memory skills:** Reading music requires visual as well as memory skills and this can put some additional burden on the visual processing system. There is evidence that some students with dyslexia may have a degree of unstable vision relating to convergence difficulties, other difficulties relating to visual sensitivity, and visual processing difficulties relating to the magnocellular visual system.
- **Visual blur and eye-tracking difficulties:** The nature of music scores with lines positioned close together can cause visual blur to occur as well as omissions and additions due to eye-tracking difficulties; indeed, in some cases the lines in a music score may close up and appear distorted.
- **Processing difficulties:** Students have to read the music score, reinterpret it for the instrument and reproduce it in a different form in the instrument being played. There are at least three simultaneous tasks in that activity, and these will present some difficulties for the student with dyslexia and impose a burden on working memory. Additionally, these activities have to be carried out at some speed, and processing speed difficulties are often characteristic of dyslexia.

- **Simultaneous processing activities occurring at once:** The student has to keep in time with other instruments in the orchestra and, perhaps, also watch the conductor. There are, therefore, considerable simultaneous processing activities occurring when the student with dyslexia is reading music and playing an instrument at the same time.
- **Coordination difficulties:** These can also affect the performance of the student.

It is important to encourage the student to adopt the strategies that suit them best. This is another way of encouraging students to self-assess and to reflect on their own learning. This is both an assessment and intervention tool.

Physical education: barriers to learning

Dyslexia and dyspraxia (developmental coordination difficulties) can often overlap, and students who experience these difficulties often face very real challenges in PE. These difficulties can be assessed informally if one knows what to look for. In some primary schools, classroom teachers may be responsible for PE lessons so it is important that all teachers and not just PE specialists know what to look for.

Classroom teachers therefore need to be encouraged to develop and utilise their own observational frameworks for pupils, which may include answers to the following questions:

- What types of tasks does the pupil find difficult?
- What types of tasks does the pupil avoid?
- Is there a physical, sensory or comprehension component to those tasks?
- Are attention problems linked to specific activities?
- Does the pupil appear to understand the instructions?
- At what point do the difficulties occur (e.g. at the start of the task or midway through)? Or is the task or activity not fully completed in the way that it was explained to the child?

Being aware of these challenges at an early stage can prevent the pupil from skipping PE lessons by feigning illness, or from losing self-esteem and feeling inadequate compared to others.

Macintyre (2009) provides clear guidance on the areas that should be targeted in an observation schedule in the early years in relation to movement and coordination issues. She suggests one needs to look at coordination, ball control (throwing and catching), balance and posture, and playground activities such as hopping and skipping.

Without early intervention or appropriate intervention, many children with motor skill deficits will have these deficits for several years. Difficulties in motor skills usually do not remediate themselves spontaneously. Avoiding or ignoring motor deficits may negatively impact on the reading and writing abilities of many students.

Overall framework that can be used with differentiation

The checklists on the next page indicate the characteristics of the difficulties that can be identified using differentiation in both primary and secondary schools. It is also important to note the frequency of these and to provide examples.

Primary school checklist

Fig. 6.2: Characteristics of difficulties that can be identified using differentiation in primary schools

Characteristic	Frequency	Examples	Support needed
Poor reading fluency			
Difficulty decoding new words			
Poor knowledge of the sounds of words			
Spelling difficulty			
Frustration			
Attention and concentration difficulties			
Discrepancies between oral and written work			

Secondary school checklist

Fig. 6.3: Characteristics of difficulties that can be identified using differentiation in secondary schools

Characteristic	Frequency	Examples	Support needed
Takes a long time over homework			
Misreads words			
Poor general knowledge			
Takes longer than most in the class on written tasks			
May not write a lot in comparison to his or her knowledge on the subject			
Difficulty copying from books			
May not finish classwork or examinations because runs out of time			

Summary

This chapter has focused on the role of differentiation in both accessing the curriculum for students with dyslexia and how this can be used to assist in the assessment process. The view advocated in this chapter is that assessment should be a learning experience and not a testing one! That is why some key assessment points can be identified within areas of the curriculum and it is important to take account of these in different subjects. In order to achieve this all staff in the school need to have an awareness of dyslexia and will therefore need training.

7 Assessment across the curriculum

Chapter overview

This chapter will:

- look at examples of curriculum-based assessment
- look at the role and nature of metacognitive assessment
- look at the role of metacognition in learning
- link assessment with teaching
- provide a framework for assessment across the curriculum
- discuss factors in literacy acquisition
- discuss a 'concern, evidence, plan, action' formula
- discuss some of the key issues in curriculum assessment.

Curriculum-based assessment

Curriculum-based assessment involves the collection of repeated short samples of a student's work within one or more curriculum areas and is applicable to primary and secondary sectors. The data collected can be used to inform planning decisions. In assessment, teachers have a dual role, which includes both selecting the assessment criteria and collecting assessment data. Compared to traditional models of educational assessment, curriculum-based assessment has the advantage that assessment is directly related to the teachers and teaching and this can help with structuring and developing the curriculum to be taught and the methods of teaching. It can also help to pinpoint different forms of assessing competence and whether the learning outcomes have been achieved.

At the same time, because curriculum-based assessment involves frequent testing, this can provide specific feedback to students and help them become aware of their progress and achieve goals.

Curriculum-based assessment can also be used to confirm standardised individual achievement test results but as an added bonus it can be related directly to curriculum materials and the nature of the errors made by the student. This can be helpful in the development of an individual education plan (IEP).

Metacognitive assessment

Metacognitive assessment essentially relates to how the child learns and how he or she is aware of this learning. It looks at the steps in learning and how the learner deals with each of these steps. By tapping into this the teacher can help the child learn more efficiently and more effectively.

The teacher has an instrumental role to play in developing metacognitive awareness and this needs to be an integral component when preparing assessment materials and also when developing the links between assessment and teaching.

Metacognition encourages students to think about the actual processes of learning in more detail. The difficulties may not lie with the child, but with an assessment process that is unable to accommodate to the diversity of different learners. Standardised tests are very prescriptive and not very flexible so they cannot be adapted to different contexts or different types of student learning preferences. For example, many students with dyslexia have more difficulty with standardised assessment as they may need more cues than the test permits.

Metacognitive assessment can be advantageous if teaching and assessment are differentiated and diversified to accommodate to differences in the student population and the school curriculum. For example, in one well-established mathematics test there are items on multiplication, which are standardised by age range, and it is expected that eight-year-old pupils will have learnt how to do multiplication. Yet I clearly recall an eight-year-old I tested indicating that he had not yet started multiplication. His score on the standardised test was therefore not a true reflection of his mathematical ability. This highlights the argument that assessment should be balanced and not totally reliant on the results of standardised tests.

Cognition and assessment

Cognition is the thinking and the reasoning stage of information processing. This refers to the information processing cycle of input, cognition and output. The cognition is the thinking part of the process and relies on a number of skills and the level of the child's background knowledge and understanding. When helping the child develop cognition it is important to:

- encourage organisational strategies to help the student become more aware of the steps in tackling a particular task
- help the student organise the new information to be learned into meaningful chunks or categories
- relate the new information to previous knowledge to ensure that concepts are clearly understood
- place the information into a meaningful framework
- help the student develop specific memory strategies, such as mind mapping (see box opposite) and mnemonics to help recall.

These points can all be assessed within the curriculum although there are standardised tests that primarily focus on cognition, such as the Wechsler Intelligence Scale (WISC-V), which was described in Chapter 4 (page 45), and the Wide Range Intelligence Test (WRIT) by Glutting et al. (2000) (see Online Resources for more information). As indicated previously, a balance between standarised, norm-referenced tests and curriculum-based assessment needs to be prioritised.

Dynamic tests

Dynamic-type testing can be related to metacognitive assessment. Essentially it emphasises the student's potential for change. Such tests do not attempt to assess how much improvement has taken place, but rather how much help students need to reach a specified criterion and how much help they will need to transfer this to novel situations. Such tests are therefore metacognitive in that they can provide information on how the student is learning.

Mind mapping

Mind mapping is a memory technique that can help the learner organise a vast amount of information into a visual format in order to make recall easier.

A mistake a lot of students make is to be too ambitious too soon. It is best to start a mind map with something very familiar, such as events that have been recently experienced or a film the student has recently seen.

An example is shown below:

Example - My weekend

1. Start with brainstorming all the things you did at the weekend.
2. Place them under categories such as: family, friends, school, recreation, other things.
3. Now make a central image in the middle of the page. This could be a drawing representing the phrase 'my weekend' or of you.
4. Now place all the categories around the image.
5. Now extend each of the categories into subcategories. For friends, for example, you may have subcategories such as activities with friends, where they took place, conversations, etc.
6. Each of these subcategories can then be subdivided into other headings. 'Activities with friends' can be divided into sport, cinema, etc. and for cinema the specific film could be another subheading.
7. Finally, once all the information has been put down into a mind map, additional images can be made to represent the words. These need not be works of art; they just need to make sense to you.

The idea is that it helps the student remember the information and organise it for easier recall. It is also good practice in lateral thinking as it helps the student make connections.

Tony Buzan has been very influential in making the technique of mind mapping well known, particularly in schools. He explains the process in the following video clip: www.youtube.com/watch?v=MlabrW v25qQ

Resources on mind mapping can be found at this link: www.thinkbuzan.com/intl/?utm_nooverride=1&gclid=CLD09tnHhK0CFQduhwodh Fp7Lw

Dynamic assessment is carried out in the following way:

1. The teacher notes the cues necessary to facilitate the correct response from the student, for example visual cues or discussion.

2. The teacher then notes information on how the student processes, thinks and essentially learns. This can be done by looking at the student's working – in maths, for example – or asking the student to think aloud or to tell you how he/she carried out the task.

3. This information can be relayed back to the student to illustrate how he or she managed to obtain the correct response.

4. As a result, the student collects information about how he or she learns best and the teacher can use this information to inform planning. This makes assessment a learning experience, not a testing one.

The role of metacognition in learning

The role of metacognition in learning is of great importance as this relates to the learner's awareness of thinking and learning. Tunmer and Chapman (1996) have shown how students with dyslexia can have poor metacognitive awareness and this can lead them to adopt inappropriate learning habits in reading and spelling. This makes the learning process ineffective and inefficient, which therefore makes it difficult for them to correct habitual mistakes. It is important that students reflect on their responses and are able to self-correct. The assessment procedure in the Reading Recovery programme is excellent for self-correction as it indicates that this means the student is operating at a higher level (see www.readingrecoveryworks.org).

As indicated above, dynamic assessment is metacognitive and this can promote reflection and help the student become more aware of his or her own learning.

Metacognitive strategies

The use of metacognitive strategies can help to develop all learning skills and can be used specifically with reading comprehension and expressive writing skills. Some specific metacognitive strategies include:

- **Visual imagery:** Discussing and sketching images from text. The student can develop a visual image and then discuss that image. This helps to link visual skills with language skills and also helps the learner to think about what he or she is learning.

- **Summary sentences:** Identifying the main ideas in text – getting the student to make summaries of what he or she has written. This can help the teacher work out whether the student is able to identify the key points. It is perhaps a good idea to do this orally to begin with and then transfer this to written work.

- **Webbing:** The use of concept maps of the ideas from a text – this can be a form of mind mapping. This helps the learner organise his or her ideas and provides him or her with his or her own personal framework for understanding and retaining the new material.

- **Self-interrogation:** This involves asking questions about what the student already knows about a topic and what he or she may be expected to learn from the new passage. This is a good exercise to carry out at the beginning of a task, as it helps to set the scene about the task. It can also be carried out at the end of the task. This can help to find out how much the student has progressed with the task. This is the most frequently used approach to assess metacognitive understanding. It can also be done while the student is engaging in the activity.

Output – presentation

Training the student to use metacognitive approaches can help them become more aware of their own learning. This includes how material is presented, and it is important to help the student pay careful attention to presentation and how to present responses in an organised and structured manner. This can be done by:

- using headings and sub-headings in written work, as this will help with structure
- encouraging the use of summaries in order to identify the key points
- monitoring and assessing learning at each point in the process.

Multiple intelligences (see below) is another means of assisting the learner to become more aware of their learning and particularly their learning preferences.

Multiple intelligences

Since Howard Gardner first wrote *Frames of Mind: The Theory of Multiple Intelligences* in the early eighties (3rd edition: Gardner, 2011), the concept of intelligence and its applicability to education has been re-examined though Gardner's eight intelligences. The eight intelligences can be summarised as follows:

1. verbal/linguistic – this involves language processing
2. logical/mathematical – this is associated with scientific and deductive reasoning
3. visual/spatial – deals with visual stimuli and visual planning
4. bodily/kinaesthetic – involves the ability to express emotions and ideas in action such as drama and dancing
5. musical/rhythmic – the ability to recognise rhythmic and tonal patterns
6. interpersonal intelligence – involves social skills and working in groups
7. intrapersonal – involves metacognitive-type activities and reflection
8. naturalist intelligence – this relates to one's appreciation of the natural world around us, the ability to enjoy nature and to classify, for example, different species of flora, and how we incorporate and react emotionally to natural environmental factors such as flowers, plants and animals.

Each of the eight intelligences can be incorporated into assessment and teaching. Multiple intelligences essentially turns the concept of 'deficit' on its head. The multiple intelligence paradigm integrated into the curriculum can include: creative writing, poetry, verbal debate and storytelling as a means of assessing the verbal–linguistic modality. It can also relate to metacognitive assessment that can provide information about a student's actual levels of understanding, and can be used to develop effective teaching approaches for students, therefore strengthening the link between assessment and teaching.

Linking assessment with teaching of literacy

Literacy is a key area in the assessment for dyslexia, and the relationship between dyslexia and literacy is discussed here. Some of the principles in intervention for dyslexia, such as over-learning, multisensory and acquiring automaticity, are discussed below in addition to some key factors in the acquisition of literacy.

Multisensory approach

There are a considerable number of intervention strategies for teaching reading and spelling to children with dyslexia. Many of these incorporate elements of what can be described as good teaching and are normally of a multisensory nature. That is, they incorporate visual, auditory, kinaesthetic and tactile elements. This is important, as students with dyslexia often have difficulty processing information using the auditory modality (i.e. listening) and it is crucial to ensure that they receive teaching input through their stronger modalities. Children with dyslexia are usually stronger in the visual and kinaesthetic modalities.

Kinaesthetic activities in particular are important as these can help the learner gain experiences in learning. This can be through drama, poetry or field trips and excursions, but it is important that the 'experience' is relevant and the learner needs to be active and participate fully throughout. It is important therefore to assess students informally using a range of modality strategies.

Learning preference

It is important to obtain information on the learner's preferences for learning styles and take these into account in teaching.

Fig. 7.1 below can be used for guidance on how to translate this into a teaching programme.

Fig. 7.1: Tasks for different learning styles (adapted from Reid and Green, 2016)

Learning style	Task
Auditory	Make lists Find out information
Visual	Drawings and diagrams Use DVD or computer programmes
Kinaesthetic	Arrange visits, activities and field trips
Persistent	Lengthy tasks Problem-solving activities
Global	Overview Short tasks Frequent breaks Discussion
Social	Work in group or pairs Discussion
Metacognitive	Problem-solving Thinking skills
Tactile	Hands-on Making models Demonstration

Over-learning

Children with dyslexia require considerable over-learning. This does not mean pure repetition of teaching through repetitive rehearsal, but rather the use of a range of teaching approaches to ensure that the same words or skills are being taught in different situations. If a new word is to be learnt, then it is important that the new word is used in other contexts and the connections are deliberately made, and that they are made clear to the learner. This also applies to spelling rules, and many spelling patterns can lend themselves quite easily to over-learning through noting similar patterns in different words.

Automaticity

One of the reasons why over-learning is an important element is that students with dyslexia often take longer than some other students to achieve automaticity. The term 'automaticity' refers to the consolidation of skills that learners normally achieve through practice. It is suggested that students with dyslexia take a longer period of time and require more varied input than some other students to acquire automaticity. This can become clear when, after a period of teaching a particular word or skill, the learner may still not have acquired mastery in that skill. This can be particularly the case if there is a break such as a holiday or even the weekend, when the word and the skills associated with the word have not been used. This is one of the reasons why dyslexic students need a considerable amount of practice in reading, including material that is below their reading age. Difficulties in acquiring automaticity can be a good assessment point and should be noted.

Factors in literacy acquisition

The factors in literacy acquisition can be examined through standardised assessment or through observation. Observation can be very powerful as it is flexible and can be contextualised to different learning and curriculum contexts. The factors include:

Auditory factors

- recognition of letter sounds
- recognition of sounds and letter groups or patterns
- sequencing of sounds
- discriminating sounds from other sounds
- discriminating sounds within words.

Linguistic factors

- the fact that the flow of oral language does not always make the break between words clear
- retaining the sounds in memory
- articulating sounds
- recognising the sounds in written form.

Visual factors

- recognising the visual cues of letters and words
- familiarity with left–right orientation
- recognising word patterns
- recognising letter and word shapes.

Contextual factors

- acquiring knowledge of vocabulary
- acquiring general knowledge
- using context as an aid to word recognition, comprehension and analogy of skills.

Developing an observation schedule

Developing an observation schedule (which can be done by using Appendices 4, 5 and 6) can be a useful way of incorporating these points. It is important to consider the point made by Bell and McLean (2016), who suggest that in the mainstream classroom, it can be easy to miss signs of specific learning difficulties, particularly when students disguise these with bad behaviour.

Many children and adults with dyslexia often cover up their difficulties with a number of avoidance strategies or by over-utilising their strengths.

It is also important to note the skills and procedures adopted by skilled readers. This can give insights into what the weaker reader needs to do to achieve a higher degree of competence. This can also provide a good example of metacognitive awareness in reading.

Good readers can often:

- generate questions while they read – this means they are thinking about the task while they are working on it
- monitor and resolve comprehension problems – when they do come across a puzzling statement or word, or one that does not fit what they might expect, they are able to self-reflect and resolve this puzzle
- utilise mental images as they read – they are not reading literally but visualising their own images of the text; this is a highly skilled activity but one that is necessary for competent reading
- reread when necessary – it is significant to note that good readers also need to reread and it is important that this is made clear to poorer readers too
- self-correct if an error has been made when reading – as indicated earlier in this chapter, self-correction is a very important activity and needs to be encouraged as much as possible; students may need to be taught how to self-correct.

All readers need to engage in pre-reading discussion. There is considerable evidence to suggest that pre-reading discussion can enhance reading fluency and understanding. It is also useful to ensure that the reader has a clear picture of the purpose of reading and an understanding of the text about to be read. Good readers will have that and these are important factors in effective reading.

Self-questioning skills for comprehension

Another important aspect of metacognitive skills is the ability to self-assess. This was introduced in Chapter 6 (page 69). Some students can do this quite well and are able to keep on track while they are learning, but others find it very difficult to keep on track and monitor their own progress. It is a good idea to observe the students as they are learning to note whether they are able to incorporate self-questioning and self-monitoring strategies into their learning.

Self-questioning during a task will allow learners to take more control over their own learning. It is important to try to assess the level of a learner's awareness of his or her own learning.

Linking assessment and support

Assessment should not be seen in isolation and needs to link with intervention. This section will look at assessment across the curriculum as a means of linking assessment with teaching.

Information processing

Dyslexia can be seen as a difference in how information is processed. It is important to identify strategies that can support the student at different stages of the information-processing cycle. As previously explained, the stages of the information-processing cycle can relate to input, cognition and output. Cognition refers to thinking and processing information and students with dyslexia may experience difficulties at any, or each, of these stages, including the cognition stage. Some suggestions for practical strategies for dealing with each of these stages can include:

Input

- present information in small units
- support to monitor comprehension – this can also involve encouraging self-questioning, particularly for students further up the school
- ensure over-learning takes place – it is important to vary the range of materials and the strategies used.

These points can help to ensure that the information is being processed by the student.

Below is a framework that can be used across the curriculum. This can provide some general pointers but can be contextualised to different subjects and curriculum areas. It is essentially continuous assessment and helps to build up a profile of the student that can be placed against the criteria for identifying dyslexia.

A framework for assessment across the curriculum

The process of assessment

1. What do I already know?
2. What else do I need to know to inform the assessment and intervention?
3. Where am I going to obtain this information?
4. What tests and other procedures will I use?
5. What else will be helpful – information from parents?
6. Do the results of the assessment inform my teaching? Can they help in the development of an IEP?
7. What procedures and measures should I use to monitor progress?

Obtaining information and evidence

1. Talking with pupils, parents and teachers.
2. Observing the student's actions.

3. Looking at the student's work for:

- general attitude
- level of concentration
- level of perseverance
- ability to do the task
- ability to interact with peers
- skills: literacy, numeracy, gross and fine motor control.

4. Testing

- standardised
- criterion-referenced
- diagnostic
- curriculum.

5. Records

- pupil self-assessment
- early years/primary/secondary records, e.g. baseline
- subject or department/team
- learning support team
- support services or psychological service.

6. Liaison

- with parents
- with specialist special needs teachers
- with external agencies.

7. How useful is the information?

- Is it up to date? Are there gaps?
- Is it valid? Is it relevant? Is it useful?
- Is it available? Does it exist? Does it need restricted access?
- Is it comprehensive? Is it manageable – too much or too little?
- Is it analytical enough?
- Does it tell you what a student can do?

Clarifying concern

The information gathered in the framework may result in concern being raised about a particular student or students. In this case, further observation and curriculum assessment can take place. It may also be useful at this stage to conduct standardised assessments but these can easily take place after more curriculum data has been obtained.

Fig. 7.2 (below) and Fig 7.3 (on the next page) can help to provide some guidance with this. See also Appendix 7: Record of concern (page 145).

Fig. 7.2: Concern, evidence, plan, action (adapted from Came and Reid, 2006)

Concern What are the difficulties? What is the impact of the difficulties on the student? Are there curricular implications? What has already been tried to support the student and help to deal with the difficulties?	**Evidence** How do we know these are the difficulties? What tests/assessment strategies have been used? What further tests/strategies can be used?
Planning intervention What are the key areas that can be implemented into a teaching programme? Which areas of the curriculum are affected by the student's difficulties? What would be the short-term plans, medium-term plans and the long-term plans for intervention? Ensure that wide consultation has taken place with the student, parents, colleagues and management (if appropriate).	**Action and review** Who is responsible for administering the plan? What are the plans for review? Who, when and how? How is progress to be measured? If progress is not evident, what action will be taken – review objectives, more time, less demanding targets? If the targets are met and progression is noted, what will be the future targets?

Assessment across the curriculum – advantages

Curriculum assessment provides opportunities for teachers to become reflective practitioners. This means that it can provide the means for all teachers in primary, secondary, FE and HE to develop skills in identifying needs. They will be able to notice what is different or unusual about patterns of progress in student learning. It also helps them to reflect more on their own teaching and what they should or can do differently to respond to the thinking of each student.

It is then possible to provide a different kind of feedback to the student. For example, the feedback can:

- focus on the tasks and the processes involved in learning and not necessarily the student difficulties

- confirm that the student is on the right track – this can help with self-monitoring and self-assessment

- include suggestions that help the student become a more effective learner and help them to recognise the scaffolds (supports) that can help with their learning

- happen all the time, which makes assessment an integral part of the teaching process

- help to promote a dialogue between the student and the teacher about the learning process and the task that is being done – it also provides opportunities for the teacher to highlight any different types of methods that the learner can use

- help the student connect more directly to specific and perhaps challenging goals

- relate to the student's prior knowledge and experience and help the student build up a schema for the task, which can give him or her a platform or framework to help understand the task

- provide opportunities for the student to work with others in the class through peer learning and jointly develop and refine their learning strategies.

Fig. 7.3: Specifying the concern

Nature of concern	Information required	Possible diagnosis/further action
Reluctance to read	Is the reader reading at the correct age range? Is the book relevant and motivating? Does the student have a schema for the story? Are the background of the story and the context of the story known to the student? Does the student experience lack of confidence?	Try easier texts with vocabulary below the student's age. Try to use books with larger typeface. Possible dyslexia but further testing is necessary.
Numeracy difficulties	Can the student identify numbers readily? Check basic arithmetic – adding, subtracting, multiplying and simple divisions. Note the type of errors the student makes? Is there a processing difficulty, e.g. makes arithmetic errors? Or a difficulty in technique and understanding what is to be done? Does the student misread the symbols, e.g. adding for subtracting? Is there a difficulty in mathematical concepts (e.g. understanding what is actually being asked and how to carry out the task)? Is there a reading comprehension difficulty?	Try reading the question to the student. Provide examples for each of the tasks. Ask the student to think aloud as he or she is responding to the question. This can help to track how he or she is tackling the problem, and any inefficiency in technique and working can be discussed. Possible diagnosis of dyscalculia but further testing necessary, e.g. dyscalculia screener.
Social/emotional concerns	How does the student react in groups? Can the student be described as being socially isolated? How is the student's demeanor, e.g. happy, sad, etc.? Is the student comfortable in a one-to-one situation? Does the student enjoy and participate in extra-curricular activities? Are there signs of stress and anxiety?	Try structured group work. You can also use the SNAP behaviour assessment tool (Long and Weedon, 2017), see Chapter 2 (page 22) and Online Resources.
Organisation/memory	Poor organisation – student omits key points in written work and in homework. Student forgets to bring items to school, e.g. PE kit. Student needs a lot of repetition. Student needs help to organise written work. Student cannot find things in his or her backpack or school bag. Student has difficulty following instructions.	Further testing – possibly cognitive testing, e.g. a psychologist using the WISC-V test (see Chapter 4) or teachers testing using WIAT-T or WIST (see Online Resources).
Attention	Student is easily distracted irrespective of what he or she is doing. Needs information to be repeated. Needs a lot of mobility and can be impulsive. Can become frustrated easily.	Further testing – use tests for ADHD (see Chapter 9). Can be associated with dyslexia or dyspraxia – or can be attention difficulties (ADHD or ADD).

Assessment across the curriculum – key issues

Some of the key issues relating to assessing for dyslexia across the curriculum include the following:

- **Assessment strategies:** It is important to use a wide range of assessment strategies and it is also important that these can link to intervention.
- **The learner:** It is also important that the needs and learning preferences of the learner are acknowledged.
- **Learning styles:** Considering the above point it is important to acknowledge that new learning materials need to be presented in a manner that can suit the student's learning style. The assessment should reveal information about the student's particular learning preferences.
- **Metacognitive factors:** These need to be considered and every effort should be made to help the student become more aware of his or her own learning and to self-monitor his or her own progress when tackling a task.
- **The subject content:** This was discussed in Chapter 6 regarding differentiation (page 67), and it is crucial if assessment is to be conducted across the curriculum that the subject content is accessible.
- **Subject delivery:** The assessment should ensure that the topics are delivered in an appropriate manner for the student with dyslexia. It is important to recognise that by doing this, it is likely to help all learners. This is because by presenting information in a dyslexia-friendly manner, it is likely that all students will in some way tap into the different modalities used in the presentation. The teacher is ensuring that the presentation of the curriculum acknowledges the specific challenges and the learning preferences as well as the strengths of students.

This can help to take into account the potential difficulties children with dyslexia may experience, but also acknowledge their strengths, and this can help to provide a positive way forward, making assessment a learning experience for all – teachers, parents and the young person being assessed.

Summary

This chapter has focused on curriculum-based assessment as a means of complementing information gleaned from standardised tests. It has also referred to metacognitive assessment as a means of gaining insights into how the learner learns. This can pave the way for more effective intervention and can also help the learner become more aware of his or her own learning preferences. Linking assessment with teaching is important and aspects of this have been addressed in this chapter. Some key factors in literacy acquisition have also been noted. Curriculum assessment helps to contextualise the needs of the student and can clarify exactly which areas of the curriculum are proving to be challenging.

Part 3 will focus on a number of issues that can impact on the learner and on the dyslexia assessment, such as social and emotional factors and those pertaining to second language learners. The overlap between dyslexia and a number of related syndromes, such as dyspraxia and dyscalculia, will also be discussed.

PART 3

Issues

8 Social, motivational and emotional factors

Chapter overview

This chapter will discuss the following factors that might affect attainment in pupils and students:

- social
- motivational
- emotional.

Social factors

Bronfenbrenner's ecological systems theory (Bronfenbrenner, 1977) provides a useful framework that helps us to consider how social factors might influence a person's development.

The theory is represented graphically by a series of five circles within circles. The first, innermost circle represents the individual, who is at the core of this conceptual model. The individual is surrounded by outside influences, starting with people close and known to the individual, and moving outwards to more abstract, societal influences.

In Bronfenbrenner's model, there are five main elements:

- the individual
- the micro-system
- the meso-system
- the exo-system
- the macro-system.

The core, 'individual' circle is surrounded by the second circle, the 'micro-system'. Both of these circles are contained within the third circle, which represents the 'meso-system'. The fourth circle, the 'exo-system', surrounds the meso-system. Finally, the 'macro-system' forms the fifth and outermost circle that encompasses them all (the exo-, meso- and micro-systems and the individual). These different categories of influence are further described and discussed below in relation to educational attainment.

- **Individual level:** We can consider internal, biological factors such as sex, age, health, etc.
- **Micro-system:** This represents people and institutions that are part of that student's life, e.g. family, friends, school, college, university.

- **Meso-system:** This describes the network of connections and interactions between the different micro-systems. This could include, for example, relationships between, on the one hand, the individual and his or her family and, on the other hand, teachers, tutors, school, college or university.

- **Exo-system:** This has a less direct but nevertheless important impact on the individual. It might include institutions that affect those to whom the individual is connected in the micro-system. For example, neighbours, local politics, social services, industry and the mass media can influence parents, carers, friends or family, and these influences can in turn affect the life of the individual.

- **Macro-system:** This describes the broader culture in which an individual lives. It is something less tangible, and because of that its effects can be extremely powerful. This is because we are often not aware of the extent to which we are influenced by cultural values that emerge as a result of our socio-economic status, ethnicity, belief systems, etc.

According to Bronfenbrenner, each of the systems in his model is characterised by rules, norms and roles, and these can shape the psychological development of the individual.

The ecological systems theory, like any model of human behaviour, can be criticised because it could not possibly capture all of the nuances of experience and influences on every individual's development. For example, even at the individual level, concepts such as sex, age and health are not simply biological. External factors affect the way we view, understand and negotiate all of them. We know this because sex, age and health are conceptualised differently across cultures and across time. The notion of a broader culture is also problematic – we might see ourselves as part of many cultural groups, and these groups might have overlapping or apparently opposing values.

However, Bronfenbrenner's theory encourages us to systematically consider the many layers, levels and networks that can influence the pupil or student. Some examples are provided below, but these are not exhaustive. The key message here is: when we are assessing for dyslexia, we need to remember that the individual we are working with is located in a series of contexts. So, we should consider a very wide picture, and not just factors within the individual.

Individual level considerations

At the individual level, we should think about the possible impact of being male, female or transgender on that individual's educational attainment. For example, there is a body of research that suggests that males might have better visuo-spatial skills than females, and that females might be stronger linguistically. This knowledge is important, because it might tell us something about the individual's likely pattern of abilities, and it might also give an indication of gender-based expectations. We need to be alert to the fact that many pupils and students will have skills that do not reflect this pattern, and consider the challenges that this could present. Social influences are discussed in more detail below.

Educational stages of development are associated with age, so this will be an important factor in terms of what is expected of that individual. Health clearly has an impact on education, and some consideration needs to be paid to things such as rate of absence, or lack of stamina to cope with the day-to-day demands of education.

Micro-system and meso-system level considerations

Roles, norms and rules affect the individual at the micro-system level, where he or she comes into contact with family, carers, friends, school, college or university. It is useful here to consider what

Mischel (1973) first described as 'social learning'. This means that we need to take account of the wider impact of family, social and broader cultural influences. For example, if certain behaviours are encouraged within a particular family, group or culture then these behaviours are likely to seem like the natural thing to do. The individual is likely to be affected by the level and nature of expectations placed on them by family or carers and by friends. For example, it is not always easy to be the first in the family to have gone on to further or higher education. It can similarly be difficult for the individual who feels that he or she is being compared with other family members who have achieved well academically.

As noted in Chapter 2 (page 16), there is a marked genetic component to dyslexia, and this means that a parent might have experienced difficulties. This could affect how the parent views educational institutions, and the ambitions that the parent has for his or her child. There can also be peer pressure to do well – or not to carry out the work required. Expectations from the individual's institution can also have an impact on the student's learning. This can be particularly problematic for dyslexic students whose difficulties might not have been identified, and especially if they have displayed behavioural difficulties that can result from frustration in the educational setting. It is hardly surprising that some teachers will have developed low expectations of pupils who are in fact capable of more – because they have not seen evidence of that student's potential.

In relation to dyslexia, the research suggests that context is very important when looking at how the individual is affected. As discussed below, dyslexia can have a negative impact on self-development and self-esteem. However, teachers and peers can have an important role in facilitating a positive sense of self in dyslexic pupils (Humphrey, 2003). In research that took place in an independent special school for dyslexic pupils, Burden and Burdett (2005) found low levels of depression and learned helplessness, and positive feelings of 'self-efficacy', 'locus of control' and 'commitment to effort' as a strategy essential to learning. (These concepts are discussed on the next page.) Emotional well-being can be enhanced through collaborative practice and whole-school, systemic work (Long et al., 2007). Casserly (2013) notes that, while the focus of academic support is on increasing literacy skills, it can also have a positive socio-emotional impact, and it can improve learners' self-confidence. The impact of educational experience at school age can extend beyond school and into adulthood (Nalvany et al., 2011).

Exo-system level considerations

At the exo-system level in Bronfenbrenner's model, we can consider how wider changes in the community might have affected the pupil or student. In practical terms, it is likely that funding issues will have had some impact on the level of educational support available to that individual. The availability of social services is also affected by the economic climate. Nearer to home, levels of employment might affect family finances.

Macro-system level considerations

Finally, we are all part of a wider culture (or many cultures), and this macro-system can affect educational attainments. For example, assumptions might be made about an individual on the basis of cultural stereotypes. Crucially, these assumptions might also be made by the pupil or student him- or herself, as well as by others – in other words, the student can self-stereotype.

It would be difficult to measure social effects on the individual, and certainly this could not be done in the course of an assessment for dyslexia. However, it is important to be aware of the nature and range of factors that could play a part in that student's educational attainments. This is crucial when we are considering how best to support learning difficulties – a large part of the solution is likely to lie in the external environment, and we should consider how that can be changed to accommodate to the individual's way of working.

Motivational factors

It is easy to imagine how the pupil's or student's level of motivation might affect his or her academic performance, and there are a number of psychological concepts and studies that can give us some insight into the factors that could be involved.

The theory of learned helplessness

In what has become a classic but controversial experiment, Seligman (1976) studied the outcome when animals were not able to make any connection between their behaviour and what happened to them. He had two groups of dogs. In each group, the dogs were given electric shocks at intervals. In one group, the dogs could escape the shock by turning it off as soon as it had started. The other dogs could not escape the shock. This was part one of the experiment. Then, in part two, the groups of dogs were put into a different situation, and this time, *both* groups had the opportunity to avoid the electric shock. The first group (who could avoid the shock in part one) learned fairly quickly how to do this in part two of the experiment. The second group did not. To recap, in the first part of the experiment, the second group had to put up with the shocks. In part two, even though they could have avoided them, they did not try. They had *learned* through their experience in part one to be helpless.

The theory of 'learned helplessness' has been used to understand the way that some people behave. That is, they might seem to be able to do something, but they do not even try. This is because they do not think they will be successful. This can be very frustrating for the teacher or parent who feels sure that the student is not working to his or her potential.

The theory of learned helplessness gives us a way of understanding that this might not be due to laziness or lack of motivation. Some active efforts might need to be made to 'unlearn' harmful past experiences, to build up that person's self-confidence.

Self-efficacy

Bandura (1977) introduced the notion of 'self-efficacy'. This is similar to self-confidence, in that it describes an individual's conviction, or expectation, that he or she can achieve a certain type of behaviour. In difficult situations, an individual's self-efficacy beliefs affect how much stress he or she feels. Self-efficacy beliefs also affect the individual's motivation to take action. Importantly, it has been shown that an individual's level of self-efficacy can be improved. The most obvious way is to have some experience of success. This experience can be drawn upon to make the individual feel more capable in future times of difficulty.

The theory of self-efficacy shows the importance of positive affirmation and encouragement. With students, it is also crucial to take small steps that are likely to be achievable, rather than to present the student with a task that seems overwhelming. The reason for this is that small steps are more likely to lead to success. This boosts self-confidence and increases feelings of self-efficacy.

Locus of control

Rotter's theory of 'locus of control' (1966) is related to self-efficacy. This theory can shed some light on how the individual might tend to have a more active or a more passive approach to learning.

As a result of earlier experiences, some people come to believe, broadly speaking, that what happens to them is the result of their own actions. These people are likely to see success as the result of their own hard work, and they are likely to take responsibility for any failures to achieve. They would be described as having an 'internal locus of control'. At the other extreme are people who have an 'external locus of control', who might be more fatalistic, holding other people responsible for things that happen to them.

Locus of control theory suggests that it is important to consider whether the individual sees him- or herself as an active and independent learner, and also whether he or she sees the value in accepting the support of others where this might be helpful. These are areas that could be explored in a pre-assessment interview.

Fear avoidance

The notion of fear avoidance has been used to shed light on the behaviour of people suffering chronic pain. It might also help to shed light on the behaviour of some learners. Fear avoidance describes a situation in which a person does not do something because he or she is worried that the experience *might* be unpleasant – and not necessarily because it is unpleasant. It has been suggested that avoidance behaviour reduces the individual's sense of control over whatever is being avoided, so this is linked to locus of control. As well as this, by trying to avoid what he or she thinks will be unpleasant, the individual never gets the chance to see that the activity is possible, and might even be enjoyable. So, fear avoidance can also have an effect on self-efficacy.

We have spoken to many pupils and students who would agree that they would rather not try something, than try it and possibly fail. This often becomes apparent in the course of an assessment, because there can be less opportunity to avoid a task, or it is perhaps more obvious in a one-to-one setting that avoidance tactics are being used. In younger pupils, this can take the form of changing the subject, delaying or downright refusal. Older students are often more subtle in their approach!

Attribution theory

Attribution theory provides another way of conceptualising the relationship between the individual and his or her actions. Heider (1958) suggested that people are naturally inclined to look for explanations of things that happen in the social world, and that these explanations can be understood in terms of attributions. That is, broadly speaking, we attribute the causes of behaviour (our own, and that of others), as either 'internal' or 'external'. Our attributions can to some extent be seen as self-serving. So, for example, we are likely to attribute someone else's behaviour as internal – to do with his or her personality, motives or beliefs. When we think about our own behaviour we are more likely to attribute it more to external factors, such as the influence of the environment, or that particular situation. In a sense, it is as if we see our own behaviour as more nuanced and responsive to external influences. This can usefully dilute our own personal responsibility for actions that could be criticised.

Attribution theory has been explored and developed over the years. Weiner (1972) used it to understand how our attributions of achievement might affect our future motivation. The logic here would be: if we attribute achievement to our own efforts, then this will be motivating to us in terms of individual growth and development. This will not happen, though, if we see our achievements as attributable to external factors. That is, there is not much point in working if we think that our previous success was due to the help that we had from others. This underlines the importance of encouraging pupils and students to become independent learners, and to feel that they can take credit for their achievements.

Weiner's attribution theory is similar to the notions of internal and external locus of control discussed above. The point with attribution theory, though, is not so much whether the individual feels *able* to take an active role. Instead, it is whether the individual feels that his or her actions were important in his or her success. For example, we could have a situation in which an individual has in fact had an active part in achieving success, but where he or she does not see it that way – the credit for that success is attributed to others. In this situation, the success does not provide the incentive or motivation that we would otherwise expect.

Burden (2008) suggests that attribution theory can help us to understand how learners with dyslexic difficulties develop a positive or negative sense of identity. He suggests that our attributions, and the confidence we have in our ability to succeed, are crucial in the learning process. He developed the 'Myself-As-Learner Scale' (MALS) – a questionnaire that can be used to help us to understand how pupils view their learning abilities (Burden, 1998). This is a 20-item, standardised scale, originally applicable to students aged nine to 16. The questionnaire was later extended for younger children and older students (Burden, 2014).

Emotional factors

Often, information gathered pre-assessment will provide an indication of possible emotional challenges. For example, a pupil or student might have experienced difficulties with anger management. He or she might have suffered from anxiety and/or depression. We need to consider how these difficulties can affect academic performance. It is also very important to bear in mind that an individual's literacy or academic difficulties could very well *lead to* emotional problems. This is discussed below, with particular reference to dyslexia.

At school level (ages eight to 15 years), Humphrey and Mullins (2002) found marked differences between the self-concept and self-esteem of dyslexic pupils, and pupils without learning difficulties. Dyslexic pupils felt isolated and excluded, and nearly half of them reported being regularly teased or bullied. Terras et al. (2009) considered the association between, on the one hand, self-esteem and, on the other hand, social, emotional and behavioural difficulties in dyslexic pupils. They found that 'social, emotional and behavioural difficulties were significantly higher [in the dyslexic pupils] than in the general population and were correlated with self-esteem' (p. 304). It seems, then, that dyslexia can lead to difficulties with self-concept and self-esteem, and that these difficulties could in turn lead to social, emotional and behavioural problems.

These difficulties are also apparent post-school. In a matched-control study carried out by Riddick et al. (1999), dyslexic students self-reported lower self-esteem than their peers. The dyslexic students' questionnaire responses indicated that they had been more anxious when at school, and that they continued to feel less competent in their written work and academic achievements. Carroll and Iles (2006) carried out a study with dyslexic HE students, and found that their anxiety levels were higher than those of students without learning difficulties. Of particular note is their finding that this anxiety was not limited to academic tasks; it extended beyond that to many social situations.

At this point, it is useful to consider why dyslexic pupils and students might have difficulties in relation to their self-esteem. Certainly, in our experience, dyslexic people often talk about the frustration of not always being able to demonstrate their abilities in academic work. This frustration is often made worse when the individual compares him- or herself with peers. This can often bring about confusing feelings, e.g. 'Why do I find this so difficult when I feel like I am just as smart as they are?' and 'Maybe I'm not that smart – if I was, I would be able to do better.' Festinger (1957) proposed a theory of 'cognitive dissonance' that explains how conflicting attitudes or beliefs can cause feelings of discomfort and unease, and that these can be a threat to the individual's concept of self.

Cognitive dissonance can sometimes lead to 'maladaptive' behaviour – that is, behaviour that is not, in the long run, in the student's own best interests. For example, he or she might avoid tasks that are likely to be hard or that might expose areas of difficulty. This means that the assessment has to be handled with sensitivity. Candidates often need some reassurance and encouragement to try or to continue with a task.

Notions of cognitive dissonance also demonstrate how the individual's social context can have an impact on learning, as discussed above. With particular reference to dyslexic learners, Glazzard (2010) studied the kinds of factors that might affect self-esteem. Teachers, peers and family were found to have an important impact. However, the most significant factor was a positive 'diagnosis' of dyslexia, and 'ownership' of the label. So, when carrying out an assessment we should also think about the impact of being given this 'label' (or of not being given a label).

There has been a great deal of research into the possible consequences of labelling. Although the label of 'dyslexia' can lead to stigmatisation, this is not always the case. For example, some people are stigmatised when there has been no formal labelling, or before labelling. This suggests that the label is not necessarily the catalyst. It could be argued that having a legitimate reason for learning difficulties might take some of the burden away; difficulties are due to dyslexia, and not due to the student's work ethic, or other factors within his or her control. Malpas (2017) interviewed adults with dyslexia or related SpLDs, to find out which characteristics were helpful. One of her findings was that understanding that you are dyslexic is important to self-esteem.

In our experience, it is very common for people to say that they feel relieved to have an explanation of what might be at the root of their difficulties. Even more importantly, this explanation should be framed in a way so that the pupil or student can see where his or her strengths are, and that this knowledge can help to design strategies that are tailored to help him or her to demonstrate these abilities.

Summary

This chapter has discussed the social, motivational and emotional factors that we should consider when carrying out an assessment. The next chapter will discuss overlapping conditions that also need to be taken into account when assessing for dyslexia.

9 Overlapping conditions

Chapter overview

This chapter will:

- look at a range of other SpLDs that can overlap with dyslexia
- define the features of other SpLDs to help dyslexia assessors to identify them during observations
- consider how other SpLDs could affect the academic performance of a pupil or student and the course of their dyslexia assessment.

As discussed in Chapter 2 (page 20), there is a growing body of research showing significant areas of overlap between a range of SpLDs. When assessing students, it is therefore important to be aware of the ways in which other SpLDs could affect the pupil or student, in academic performance and during the course of his or her assessment.

This chapter will discuss these issues in relation to the following conditions:

- attention deficit disorder (ADD) and attention deficit hyperactivity disorder (ADHD)
- auditory processing disorder (APD), also known as central auditory processing disorder (CAPD)
- visual stress
- maths learning difficulties (MLD) and dyscalculia
- dysgraphia
- dyspraxia, also known as developmental coordination disorder (DCD).

Broadly speaking, there are three aspects that we need to consider:

1. The pupil or student might not have previously been assessed with another SpLD, but results of the dyslexia assessment might suggest that there are overlapping difficulties that might need to be explored further.

2. Some pupils or students coming for a dyslexia assessment will already have been assessed as having one or more SpLD. This means that we need to consider how other SpLDs might account for any literacy difficulties that are found during the assessment. That is, are the problems largely due to dyslexia, or some other SpLD?

3. We need to take account of the effects that overlapping conditions might have on the assessment itself.

This means that as assessors we need to be able to spot possible signs of overlapping conditions, how they might be related to the learning of literacy skills, and how they might affect the process of assessment. These three points will be discussed in relation to the aforementioned SpLDs.

ADD and ADHD

Signs of ADD and ADHD

The defining feature of ADD is a difficulty in maintaining attention, and there is the additional feature of physical restlessness in those with ADHD. The *Diagnostic and Statistical Manual of Mental Disorders (DSM-V)* (American Psychiatric Association, 2013) describes ADHD as:

> A persistent pattern of inattention and/or hyperactivity-impulsivity that interferes with functioning or development, as characterised by inattention and/or hyperactivity and impulsivity.

The following website has both the DSM-V criteria for ADHD and also suggestions for resources and how to deal with ADHD: www.addrc.org/dsm-5-criteria-for-adhd/

AD(H)D symptoms often improve with age, or can sometimes be more easily channelled as the pupil matures. When carrying out an assessment, we sometimes do observe signs of inattention, impulsivity and/or hyperactivity. Younger pupils might move around a lot in the chair, play with items on the desk, or get up and move around the room. In older pupils and students, the signs would often be more subtle, and might be better described as a general restlessness and difficulty in staying on-task. A full assessment of ADD/ADHD would consider the individual's behaviour in different settings, and over an extended period of time.

How might ADD or ADHD be related to literacy attainment?

The pupil who finds it difficult to maintain attention is likely to have problems with attainment in literacy. Attention difficulties could affect the ability to take in information, remember and follow instructions, and produce structured and focused work. It can be difficult to revise and to maintain focus in exams.

It would be important before or during the dyslexia assessment to ascertain whether apparent attention difficulties have been noted in the past, and the extent of any support that has been provided. For example, if a pupil has had a high level of continued support and appropriate accommodations, this could significantly mitigate the effects of ADD or ADHD. If he or she still has difficulties in literacy attainment, these might be due to dyslexia.

It can, of course, be difficult to obtain detailed and accurate information about support and accommodations, and in many cases nothing has been provided. So, we need to look for clues in the cognitive profile, and we need to be able to distinguish between the types of literacy difficulty that might and might not be due to ADD or ADHD, e.g.:

- The individual with ADD or ADHD often has a relatively low working memory (in comparison to his or her verbal and non-verbal reasoning).

- Performance in processing speed tasks can vary.

- There can generally be a tendency to work quickly, but sometimes this results in a higher level of error, which reduces the overall score.

- There might be some delay in literacy attainment, but specific weaknesses in phonological awareness would not be expected.

- Sometimes, we find that reading accuracy is good but comprehension is lower than expected, and this is related to a difficulty in maintaining focus on the text.

- Similarly, the pupil or student might be able to write well in terms of vocabulary and grammar at sentence level, but he or she might find it very difficult to produce extended written work.

How might ADD or ADHD affect the process of assessment?

If we know, or suspect, that a pupil or student has ADD or ADHD, then we might have to make some allowances for this during the course of the assessment. We will also need to keep this in mind when analysing the results of individual tests and the overall profile of scores. With younger pupils, we might need to take a bit longer to allow them to get up and move around between or during tests. Some prompting is likely to be helpful to keep the individual on-task and focused on what is being asked – although this has to be done within the rules of standardised tests. Tolerance of fidgeting and general restlessness is of course essential! We might consider using shorter texts to assess comprehension. It is important throughout the assessment to note where, and how, the signs of ADD or ADHD might have affected performance on individual tests, so that some account can be taken when carrying out the final analyses.

APD (CAPD)

Signs of APD

Individuals with APD or CAPD have difficulty in processing sounds. This can make it hard to understand speech, especially if there is background noise. They might be very sensitive to noise, and find that it is very distracting. APD can affect the ability to understand and to retain information that is given orally, and therefore to follow instructions. It can also have an impact on the individual's ability to express him- or herself in speech. The following tests may be useful:

- TAPS (Test of Auditory Processing Skills; Martin and Brownwell, 2005) can be used to assess auditory processing in pupils and students aged four to 18.
- SCAN-3:C Tests for Auditory Processing Disorders for Children (Keith, 2009) can be used with pupils aged five to 12.

How might APD be related to literacy attainment?

For the individual with APD, it can be hard to distinguish between sounds that are similar. This can have a knock-on effect on spelling and reading because there can be confusion between the sounds that make up words (phonemes). This in turn can limit the individual's vocabulary, which can affect access to the curriculum as the student progresses in his or her studies.

It would be important before or during the dyslexia assessment to find out whether APD has been identified, and if so to what extent it might have affected development of spelling and reading skills.

It is also important to look for possible indicators of APD in the cognitive profile. For example, tests that are delivered orally might be affected. These would often include tests of verbal comprehension and working memory. We would also need to consider what types of literacy difficulty might be attributed to APD, and which are less likely to be associated with this condition. As noted above, spelling and reading can be affected, and there might be difficulties with phonological awareness – there is therefore an overlap with dyslexia. An analysis of the types of spelling and reading error can be useful; it is likely that, for a student with APD, similar-sounding letters or letter blends will be confused, and that other types of mistakes are less likely to be APD-related. It is also less likely that

APD will affect performance in tests of phonological processing speed that use visual stimuli (such as rapid naming). Written expression might be characterised by spelling errors, but it might nevertheless show an ability to produce grammatical sentences and to structure extended written work.

How might APD affect the process of assessment?

If we know, or suspect, that a pupil or student has APD, then we should take this into account during the assessment and when we analyse the results of individual tests, as well as the overall profile of scores. It is particularly important to make sure that background noise is kept to a minimum. If there are any interruptions, it is important to note the duration and possible impact in relation to the test being carried out at the time. This information would inform the final analysis. It is also important that the student is asked to let the assessor know if he or she has not heard or understood an instruction. Where possible, information might need to be repeated (this is not always permitted in standardised tests). Some allowance might need to be made for expressive difficulties, and the pupil or student might benefit from some encouragement and/or prompting where this is appropriate to the test being carried out.

Visual stress

Signs of visual stress

Individuals with visual stress have difficulty processing written text. Sometimes the words or the gaps between the words appear to move, and it can be hard to track text. This can affect comprehension. It can also make reading unpleasant or tiring. If possible, it can be useful to give the pupil or student a selection of tinted overlays to see whether placing one over the text reduces the difficulty. If it does, then that overlay can then be used during the course of his or her assessment. If an overlay is found to be helpful, then a full optometrist assessment might be useful to further explore this difficulty.

How might visual stress be related to literacy attainment?

For the person with visual stress, it can be hard to accurately read single words – sometimes letters are transposed. This could have a knock-on effect on spelling, because the pupil is not consistently seeing the correct version of words.

Reading can be accurate, but slow. A lack of fluency can affect comprehension, meaning that the pupil or student has to reread in order to fully understand text. This in turn can affect the pupil's enjoyment of reading, which can limit the individual's vocabulary. This can affect access to the curriculum as the student progresses in his or her studies.

It would be important before or during the dyslexia assessment to find out whether visual stress has been identified, and if so to what extent it might have affected the development of reading and spelling skills.

We should also look for possible indicators of visual stress in the cognitive profile. For example, there might be an impact on tests that involve visual processing. These would often include tests of perceptual reasoning and processing speed. We would also need to consider what types of literacy difficulty might be attributed to visual stress, and which are less likely to be associated with this condition. As noted above, reading and spelling can be affected. An analysis of the types of error can be useful. It is likely that for the person with visual stress, letters or letter blends that look similar will be confused. Often, single letters are misread or omitted, and letters are transposed. It is unlikely that visual stress will affect performance in tests of working memory and verbal comprehension speed that use auditory stimuli. Written expression might show difficulties with handwriting and spelling errors, but the pupil might still be able to produce grammatical sentences and to structure extended written work.

How might visual stress affect the process of assessment?

If we know, or suspect, that a pupil or student has visual stress then we should take this into account during the assessment and when we analyse the results of individual tests, as well as the overall profile of scores. It is important to ask the student to let you know if symptoms of visual stress seem to be affecting performance. This can sometimes happen after extended reading, or when looking at 'busy' patterns.

Maths learning difficulties and dyscalculia

Signs of maths learning difficulties and dyscalculia

Some pupils and students have particular difficulties with mathematics, and their performance in this subject is lower than might be expected from their ability level and when compared to their work in other areas of the curriculum. Dyscalculia refers to a more fundamental difficulty in understanding number. The SpLD Working Group 2005/DfES Guidelines (www.sasc.org.uk/SASCDocuments/SpLD_Working_Group_2005-DfES_Guidelines.pdf, page 5) note the following:

Dyscalculia is a learning difficulty involving the most basic aspect of arithmetical skills. The difficulty lies in the reception, comprehension, or production of quantitative and spatial information. Students with dyscalculia may have difficulty in understanding simple number concepts, lack an intuitive grasp of numbers and have problems learning number facts and procedures. These can relate to basic concepts such as telling the time, calculating prices, handling change.

Dyscalculia differs from maths learning difficulties (MLD) because the individual who is dyscalculic has difficulties with simple number *concepts*. For example, the number 7 can represent a quantity of 7, or two quantities of 3 and 1, or a quantity of 5 and 2, etc. These are called number bonds. Someone who is dyscalculic might find that hard to grasp. They have what is described as a 'unitary' concept of number and do not always understand the concept of number bonds. Individuals with dyscalculia sometimes have difficulties with the number operations (addition, subtraction, multiplication and division). Often, they cannot remember how to carry out these operations. Another difficulty that can be experienced relates to the place value of numbers. For example, a 1 at the end of a whole number indicates 1, but a 1 before that indicates 10.

A number of tests can be used to further explore mathematics skills, including:

- the dyscalculia screener, available at: dyscalculia-screener.co.uk
- the tests that are provided in *More Trouble with Maths: A Complete Guide to Identifying and Diagnosing Mathematical Difficulties* (Chinn, 2012)
- WIAT-3 Maths and Maths Fluency (see Online Resources for more details)
- WRAT-4 Math Computation (see Online Resources for more details).

How might MLD and dyscalculia be related to literacy attainment?

If the individual being assessed has difficulties with maths, it is important to find out which areas he or she finds particularly hard. If the pupil or student can manage paper-and-pencil computations but not mental maths, this suggests that he or she has abilities in the subject and that the difficulty is likely to be related to working memory or processing speed. As we have noted in previous chapters, dyslexia is often associated with relative difficulties in working memory and/or processing speed.

It is also important to try to find out whether the pupil or student has difficulties with the language of maths. For example, does he or she find it hard to remember or to understand technical terms? Does he or she have difficulty in understanding what exactly is being asked in lengthy, worded maths problems? These types of difficulty are often associated with dyslexia – it is the reading aspect, rather than the computational aspect, that is affecting performance.

Another indicator of dyslexic difficulties can be seen in the pupil's or student's workings. Dyslexic students often misread the operator, and might therefore produce the right answer to the wrong sum! So, for example, we will see a correct addition carried out when a subtraction was required. Dyslexia can therefore be at the root of some MLDs. Dyslexia could similarly affect the student who is dyscalculic, but it is not likely to account for all of his or her difficulties with number concept.

How might MLD and dyscalculia affect the process of assessment?

If we know, or suspect, that a pupil or student has MLD or is dyscalculic, then we might have to make some allowances for this during the course of the assessment. For example, working memory is sometimes measured using mental arithmetic as a subtest. A student or pupil who is dyscalculic might not be using working memory at all because he or she is not able to attempt the calculation. (Conversely, we sometimes see pupils and students who are very skilled in this area. They carry out the computation so quickly that the task puts very little demand on their working memory, and this can result in an overall score that overstates working memory skills.) We also often find that students who have difficulties working with fractions and decimals, or more generally with shapes and rotations, etc., will also have a relative difficulty with perceptual reasoning. Perceptual reasoning gives us an indication of non-verbal reasoning, and it is possible therefore if a pupil or student is dyscalculic that this will affect the score here.

Dysgraphia

Signs of dysgraphia

Dysgraphia means difficulties with handwriting. This relates to fine motor skills and is separate from an individual's ability to express him- or herself in writing. Individuals who are dysgraphic tend to have an awkward pen or pencil grip. Their writing can look quite laboured, and often it is hard to read because the letters are badly formed, or uneven, or unevenly spaced. People who have dysgraphia can find it quite uncomfortable to write by hand. They often have difficulties in relation to their speed of handwriting. The following tests may be useful (see Online Resources for further information):

- DASH (Detailed Assessment of Handwriting) tests (Barnett et al., 2007) and DASH 17+ tests (Barnett et al., 2010) can be used to assess handwriting in pupils and students from age nine to age 25.

- The Beery-Buktenika Motor Co-ordination sixth edition (Beery VMI) test (Beery et al., 2006) can be used to examine fine motor pencil skills.

How might dysgraphia be related to literacy attainment?

Dysgraphia is likely to make it hard for the individual to keep up when taking notes, or to take notes that he or she can read later. It can also be difficult for the pupil or student to present his or her ideas effectively. Marks in tests are often lost for poor presentation, or simply because the teacher cannot decipher the script. Writing under exam conditions is particularly demanding.

It is important to find out whether the pupil or student has had access to a laptop, digital recorder or a scribe in class, or to a laptop or scribe in exams, and whether he or she has used any assistive technologies – for example, voice recognition software. These accommodations could significantly mitigate the effects of dysgraphia (providing that the pupil or student has sufficiently good keyboard skills). If we still see difficulties with written expression – for example, in relation to grammar, organisation and structure – then these are more likely to be related to dyslexia than dysgraphia.

Dysgraphia can sometimes obscure spelling – it might not be not clear whether a word has been misspelt because the legibility of the letters means they cannot always be accurately identified. It may be that a spelling difficulty has been missed, or that an assumption has been made that spelling is poor when it is not. Spelling can be affected when pupils are not able to produce cursive writing in the usual way. For example, if a letter is started in the wrong place, or is written in the wrong way, it is not possible to easily join it to the next letter. This can affect fluency in the transfer of known spelling onto paper.

How might dysgraphia affect the process of assessment?

It is important before or during the dyslexia assessment to find out whether the pupil or student has experience of using a keyboard, and if so whether he or she is faster at typing than handwriting. Also, does he or she prefer to handwrite, or to use a computer? This information will provide the context for recommendations resulting from an assessment. For example, a course in typing could be a suggestion, and we would certainly not advise using a computer in exams without sufficient skills or prior practice.

In the cognitive tests, processing speed tests often involve pencil skills. It is important to make some assessment of how dysgraphia might have affected performance. Where there is a choice, it would be preferable to opt for a test that does not involve writing.

In the literacy tests, it is useful to remind the individual being assessed (where appropriate) that spelling is not being timed, and to ask him or her to write the words as clearly as possible. Double-check the answer with the pupil or student when it is not clear. Some adjustment is likely to be needed in written expression tests. For example, deliver two versions of a test – one using a keyboard, and one written by hand. This can be tiring for the student, and will not be useful if he or she does not usually use a computer for writing. Make sure that you can read the content – it can be illuminating to ask the pupil or student to read out what he or she has written. Sometimes, the pupil or student cannot make it out either!

Dyspraxia (DCD)

Signs of dyspraxia

Dyspraxia is sometimes referred to as a developmental coordination disorder (DCD). It relates to problems with motor coordination. The following definition is taken from the SpLD Working Group 2005/DfES Guidelines (www.sasc.org.uk/SASCDocuments/SpLD_Working_Group_2005-DfES_Guidelines.pdf, page 5):

> A student with dyspraxia/DCD may have an impairment or immaturity in the organisation of movement, often appearing clumsy. Gross motor skills (related to balance and co-ordination) and fine motor skills (relating to the manipulation of objects) are hard to learn and difficult to retain and generalise. Writing is particularly laborious and keyboard skills difficult to acquire. Individuals may have difficulty organising ideas and concepts. Pronunciation may also be affected, and people with dyspraxia/DCD may be over/under sensitive to noise, light and touch. They may have poor awareness of body position and misread social cues in addition to those shared characteristics common to many SpLDs.

Macintyre and McVitty (2004), Macintyre (2012), Kirby and Rosenblum (2008) and Kirby and Drew (2017) have written extensively on how to spot the signs of dyspraxia in pupils and students, and how best to support them. The Beery-Buktenica Visual Motor Integration, Motor Co-ordination and Visual perception tests can be used to explore the separate skills of visual and fine motor skills, as well as their integration in pencil tests.

How might dyspraxia be related to literacy attainment?

The points noted above in relation to dysgraphia are likely to be relevant for those dyspraxic pupils and students who have difficulties with fine motor skills. These might affect handwriting, so that what is produced obscures spelling. The dyspraxic pupil or student might also find it difficult to organise text on paper. Notes can appear jumbled or disjointed, and work may seem disorganised on the page. These apparent difficulties with organisation can be seen in the pupil's or student's cognitive performance. Self-organisation can be difficult, and this affects the ability to be in the right place, at the right time, with the right equipment, as well as to start and to structure work. This cluster of difficulties can affect the ability to keep up in classes, to record information, to follow instructions, and to produce structured and organised work. It can be difficult to revise, and to produce work that reflects abilities in exams.

How might dyspraxia affect the process of assessment?

If we know, or suspect, that a pupil or student is dyspraxic, then we might have to make some allowances for this in the course of the assessment. It is very important to note where, and how, the signs of dyspraxia might have affected performance on individual tests, so that some account can be taken when carrying out the final analyses.

Similar difficulties are likely to be seen as noted above for pupils and students who are dysgraphic. It is also worth noting here that some dyspraxic pupils and students might find it equally hard to use a standard keyboard, and that this is not always going to be a helpful accommodation.

In the cognitive assessment, tests that involve fine motor movements, such as pencil work or handling objects, are likely to be more challenging. It is important to consider whether, for example, the test is actually measuring cognitive processing speed or perceptual reasoning, when motor skills play a significant role in the task. Dyspraxic pupils and students who have difficulties with spatial organisation can have a relative difficulty with perceptual reasoning tasks. Perceptual reasoning gives an indication of non-verbal reasoning, and it is possible therefore, if a pupil or student is dyspraxic, that this will affect the score here.

In the attainment tests, some adjustments might need to be made to take account of possible dyspraxic difficulties. As for dysgraphic pupils and students, it can be useful to remind the individual being assessed (where appropriate) that spelling is not being timed, so that he or she does not feel under pressure to work quickly. Double-check written work with the pupil or student if it is not clear.

Summary

This chapter has outlined features of ADD and ADHD, APD, visual stress, MLD and dyscalculia, dysgraphia and dyspraxia that might play a role in literacy difficulties and during the course of an assessment for dyslexia. It is worth noting that a pupil or student might display some features of more than one of these conditions, and that the assessor has to be alert to this possibility.

10 EAL: assessing dyslexia in different languages

Chapter overview

This chapter will look at issues relating to supporting pupils and students whose first language may not be English, including:

- reading and reading skills
- issues relating to dyslexia and bilingualism
- culture and the role of language experience
- assessing non-verbal intelligence
- assessment procedures that can be useful for pupils or students who are learning an additional language.

Dyslexia and bilingualism

Assessment for dyslexia should always take a holistic view and not rely solely on the results of tests, but this is particularly crucial in the case of bilingual children. Forbes and Powell (2000) strongly suggest that test materials should not discriminate against pupils and students because of their unfamiliarity with the language or language forms. They were referring to the Welsh language in particular and suggest that appropriate consideration needs to be given to design, format, language and purpose of the tests so that it is possible to develop an effective, user-friendly reading measure suitable for bilingual pupils and students.

This is an important point and is highlighted in a study by Deponio et al. (2000), which investigated the processes involved in identifying bilingual pupils who may be dyslexic. Their research suggests that bilingual learners are significantly under-represented among pupils who are assessed as having specific learning difficulties or dyslexia. This is likely due to a number of factors such as cultural norms but also the lack of availability of specific tests that can assess for dyslexia in a bilingual population.

It is important to look for indicators of dyslexia among pupils who are bilingual in the early stages. Guise et al. (2016) indicate that it is important for teachers to be alerted if:

- the pupil has a lack of interest in books
- there is a discrepancy between listening comprehension and reading skills
- the pupil has a difficulty in acquiring automaticity in skills they have learnt
- there are persistent problems in phonological awareness despite adequate exposure to English.

In relation to this, the research by Guise et al. has important implications. They indicate that dyslexia is primarily a language disorder, involving difficulties with:

- hearing and confusing sounds within words
- isolating and manipulating sounds within words
- retrieving the pronunciation of letters and groups of letters quickly
- verbal working memory, often including less-developed vocabulary skills
- word-finding difficulties.

They also state that it is reasonable to expect that when students with dyslexia are required to learn an additional language or languages, then they may very well experience difficulties. Diagnosing the causes of this – whether it is due to inadequate exposure to the language or to some other factors such as dyslexia – can be tricky.

This problem arises because there is a lack of formal tests in many languages other than English. Assessment instruments have now been translated into Spanish, Chinese and other languages but it is also important to have robust assessment procedures taking a holistic approach in the first language, because translations of a test developed initially in English may not be adequate. It is important therefore that non-biased assessment techniques and assessment tools are available in different languages, and protocols for selecting assessment tools, which can include norms that are sensitive to cultural and linguistic differences, are available.

It is important to highlight the need for culture-fair assessment (assessment that is not biased towards any one culture), and Reid and Fawcett observe that one of the areas that has gained momentum has been the acknowledgement of the need to 'promote appropriate and effective practices both in the assessment and in the intervention for students whose first language is not English.' (Reid and Fawcett, 2004, p. 13) But it needs to be noted that although there are a number of tests that contain the word 'dyslexia' in their title, there is no single dyslexia test.

Vocabulary

Specific requirements are necessary in the construction of tests aimed at second language learners. For example, Elbeheri and Everatt (2016) indicate that most studies comparing vocabulary performance of bilinguals and monolinguals conclude that bilinguals know fewer words in one of their languages compared to monolingual speakers. This means that when assessing pupils or students in their second or additional language, it needs to be noted that a test score that relies on vocabulary knowledge may be depressed when considered against scores (norms) produced by first language/monolingual speakers. This can apply to many of the tests used in a conventional battery of tests to identify dyslexia.

Pronunciation

Even within a language there can be special considerations such as pronunciation that need to be taken into account. For example, there are more than 20 countries in the Middle East region where Arabic is the official language, but there are regional variations between native speakers and therefore these differences can lead to a decrease in mutual understanding of the same basic language. This point also needs to be considered in test construction and administration. Similarly, in China there are also disparities in the spoken language across regions, and the differences between Mandarin and Cantonese are well documented. Choosing tests therefore that have been designed with a local spoken form in mind is important, but using a local pronunciation when presenting the test materials is also crucial, particularly when looking at aspects of phonological processing.

Everatt et al. (2013) argue that sensitive English assessment measures are highly predictive of skills in other languages. Nevertheless it is important to obtain measures in the pupil's first language as there will be differences in the development of different aspects of the reading process. Everatt et al. (2010) found this when undertaking research with children from the Philippines and Namibia. They found that word reading and non-word decoding developed at different rates for Filipino and Herero children in relation to English children. Despite this, it can be suggested that phonological skills are still the main predictor of children's literacy learning in both languages.

It seems that awareness of the linguistic, cultural and other background elements of the individual being assessed should collectively form a framework of dyslexia assessment.

Culture and language experience

Siegel (2016) argues that it is important to note the language experiences of the EAL pupil with peers. She suggests that it is also important to ascertain if the pupil went to a pre-school where many of the children and the teachers were native English speakers. Siegel also argues that having older siblings who speak English is a key factor and she states that if the individual plays with native English speakers in the neighbourhood, then the EAL pupil will learn a colloquial English and bring this experience to formal schooling.

This means, as Siegel states, that if reading tests or pre-reading tests are carried out with the pupil and the results are within the average range then it is unlikely they are dyslexic. She further states that on the other hand, if the pupil's performances on reading tasks are low then it is likely that they are dyslexic, providing that they have had sufficient exposure to reading instruction in English. She indicates that it is important to ascertain the nature of the child's exposure to English as this is an important determinant of a potential diagnosis of dyslexia, or even the identification of children at risk of dyslexia.

Siegel suggests that knowing the names of the letters, which is tested in a number of literacy tests, is a good predictor of subsequent reading difficulties, as is the level of the child's phonological awareness – the Comprehensive Test of Phonological Processing (CTOPP-2) can be used for this (see Chapter 4, page 42, and Online Resources). She argues that there is likely to be a large proportion of bilingual pupils who have dyslexia but as yet are undiagnosed or misdiagnosed.

Bilingualism and multilingualism are therefore areas that can present a challenge to educators and assessors and it is widely acknowledged that dyslexia can occur across languages and cultures (British Psychological Society, 1999).

As has already been noted in this chapter, cultural and language factors in many standardised tests can mitigate against the pupil whose first language is not English, as most of the standardised assessment strategies have been developed for use with a monolingual population and this can account for the underestimation or, indeed, the misdiagnosis of dyslexia in bilingual children.

Landon (2001) addressed this by asking, 'what factors appear to lead to low rates of detection of dyslexia amongst bilingual learners and could the same factors also explain the poor standards of literacy amongst many learners of English as an Additional Language (EAL learners)?' The importance of these questions is that they actually investigate the issues and provide a good example of the types of questions teachers need to ask when assessing children who are bilingual. To answer the questions presented by Landon, one must consider the range of factors that contribute to dyslexia, and it is important to acknowledge that culture-fair assessment materials need to be developed in two ways:

1. Assessment materials need to be developed in the language being taught, but to make those materials culture-fair, they may also involve a heavy visual emphasis.

2. Assessment materials need to be developed in the pupil's first language to assess whether dyslexia is present and affecting the development of skills in literacy in that first language.

Kelly (2002) suggests that teachers need to consult and collaborate with people who have a sound knowledge of the cultural background of the students, as this can avoid confusing common second-language errors of bilingual students with indicators of dyslexia. She suggests that these can sometimes overlap, as in the case of left–right confusion in Urdu, which is written from right to left, and with auditory discrimination with Punjabi speakers, who may have difficulty distinguishing 'p' from 'b'. It is important to obtain information from parents, as parents will have a more complete picture of their child in a range of different settings.

Guise and Reid (2016) suggest that when it is known that English is an additional language, we should request extra information that can inform us about the student's competence in English, and in his or her first and other languages. Specifically, we need to find out:

- What is the student's first language?
- How long has the student been speaking English?
- What other languages does the student speak?
- How much and what level of education has been in English?
- What language is spoken by the student's parents or guardians?
- What language is spoken at home, with siblings, and with friends?

Some guidance on the possible effects of the EAL HE student's exposure to English in the UK is provided by the SpLD Working Group 2005/DfES report (SASC, 2005, p. 12; www.sasc.org.uk/SASCDocuments/SpLD_Working_Group_2005-DfES_Guidelines.pdf):

> Where first exposure to English was after the age of seven, some impact on phonology and pronunciation is generally to be expected. However, much will depend on the quality and quantity of English experience during formative years.

Assessing non-verbal intelligence

It has been well documented in this chapter that linguistic aspects of an assessment for pupils and students who are bilingual can be quite tricky to implement in an assessment, mainly due to factors such as vocabulary, pronunciation and linguistic experiences. It is important nevertheless to include test items that do focus on linguistic aspects, but these should be in both first and second languages. Additionally, some caution is required when interpreting the results of the assessment, and cultural and language experiences need to be considered. It is also important however to look at non-verbal aspects.

There are several tests that can provide information on non-verbal intelligence and other non-verbal aspects, for example the visual subtests in the WISC-V, such as the fluid reasoning and visual spatial tests, as well as picture memory, which looks at visual memory. In addition, the subtests on coding and symbol search (see Online Resources for further information) are both speed tests using visual symbols or numbers. These are appropriate for bilingual students (but the WAIS-IV should be used for adults) and can provide a measure of speed of processing.

Additionally, the receptive and expressive vocabulary subtests in the WIAT-III rely on picture cues to elicit a response, although in receptive vocabulary there is a target word and in expressive vocabulary a target phrase.

The CTONI-2 can also be useful for bilingual students as it contains visual subtests measuring reasoning and sequential skills.

Building a learning profile for bilingual students

Below is a list of factors that can contribute to building a learning profile and help identify dyslexia in bilingual pupils and students.

Excellent further guidance for HE students can be obtained from the SASC (www.sasc.org.uk/SASCDocuments/REVISED%20guidelines-March%202016%20a.pdf).

1. **Blending words** – the ability to synthesise sounds to form words.

2. **Sound matching** – the ability to select words with the same initial and final sounds.

3. **Phoneme isolation** – the ability to isolate individual sounds within words.

4. **Blending nonwords** – the ability to synthesise sounds to form nonwords.

5. **Segmenting nonwords** – the ability to segment nonwords into phonemes.

6. **Memory for digits** – the ability to repeat numbers accurately.

7. **Nonword repetition** – the ability to repeat nonwords accurately.

8. **Rapid digit naming** – the ability to rapidly name numbers.

9. **Rapid letter naming** – the ability to rapidly name letters.

10. **Rapid colour naming** – the ability to rapidly name colours.

11. **Rapid object naming** – the ability to rapidly name objects.

12. **Word identification** – word reading accuracy.

13. **Reading** – reading rate, reading accuracy and reading comprehension.

14. **Spelling** – letter order and letter confusion.

15. **Writing** – the use of vocabulary and ability to use extended vocabulary.

16. **Logical sentences and story composition** – the ability to write logical sentences and compose a story.

Summary

This chapter has explored the difficulties of assessing for dyslexia in bilingual children, including the lack of assessment tools that are available in different languages and that are culture-fair. It has also noted that special considerations need to be made when assessing bilingual children, including vocabulary, pronunciation and cultural and linguistic experience. A number of factors have also been identified that teachers can look out for to help identify dyslexia in bilingual pupils and students. The next chapter will be a concluding one and will provide some research and theoretical perspectives that underpin dyslexia.

11 Conclusion

Chapter overview

This chapter will:

- discuss the current areas of research in dyslexia and the role of a definition of dyslexia
- consider government reports such as the Rose Report and DSM-V (Diagnostic Statistical Manual 5th edition)
- explore suggestions for intervention
- summarise the key points made throughout this book.

A working definition of dyslexia

In this book, we have attempted to integrate theory and practice and have focused more on practice, particularly on the view that assessment is a process that involves much more than a quick screening procedure. It is important that those conducting an assessment for dyslexia have a sound theoretical overview and therefore in this final chapter we highlight the key points and issues in dyslexia research. Research should inform assessment and intervention as well as provide pointers towards a working definition of dyslexia.

Defining dyslexia can be tricky and complex. The problem with a definition of dyslexia lies to a great extent with the lack of a universally accepted definition of dyslexia. Different countries, educational authorities, organisations and sometimes schools each may have their own definition. Despite that, there are many similar factors in different definitions and these have been indicated throughout this book in relation to detailing the assessment procedures involved in identifying dyslexia. It can be noted that although there are many different definitions of dyslexia, there are also many commonalities.

Working definition

We provided a working definition of dyslexia at the beginning of Chapter 1. The main points in this definition are:

- **Processing difference:** This highlights the differences between individuals.
- **Difficulties in literacy acquisition:** This is one of the key areas in a definition and a subsequent diagnosis of dyslexia, as it is usually these difficulties that first alert the teacher or the parent of a problem – this can and should be noted in the early years.
- **Cognitive processes:** Cognition means learning and processing information. This can be challenging for pupils and students with dyslexia and a full assessment should always include a measure of cognitive abilities. This would provide information on long-term and short-term memory, as well as working memory, processing speed and the ability to make connections and utilise prior learning. The Rose Report into dyslexia teaching (Rose, 2009) recognised this and provided a working definition that took into account a number of other characteristics such as verbal memory and processing speed.

- **Discrepancies in educational performance:** This is often one of the most obvious indicators of dyslexia. There can be a difference between the reasoning abilities (oral/verbal comprehension or visual/perceptual reasoning) and the processing performances (working memory and processing speed). This means that children and adults with dyslexia can solve problems and can reason and understand information, but they may have difficulty in processing the information accurately and using that information.

- **Individual differences:** It is important to recognise that pupils and students with dyslexia are individuals, and their individual learning preferences and differences need to be acknowledged. Not all children and adults with dyslexia will have the same profile, although they may all meet the criteria for dyslexia.

- **Strengths:** The importance of this has been indicated throughout this book – recognising strengths while undertaking an assessment is essential. Quite often pupils and students with dyslexia can be strong in the visual/kinaesthetic modalities. This means they need to see and experience the new learning.

Rose Report definition (2009)

The Rose Report from 2009 has considerable implications for dyslexia assessment, intervention and training, and a summary of the description of dyslexia adopted in the report (Rose, 2009, page 9) is as follows:

Dyslexia is a learning difficulty that primarily affects the skills involved in accurate and fluent word reading and spelling [...] phonological awareness, verbal memory and verbal processing speed [and which] occurs across the range of intellectual abilities.

The British Dyslexia Association definition

In October 2007, the BDA management board approved the following definition:

Dyslexia is a specific learning difficulty that mainly affects the development of literacy and language related skills. It is likely to be present at birth and to be life-long in its effects. It is characterised by difficulties with phonological processing, rapid naming, working memory, processing speed, and the automatic development of skills that may not match up to an individual's other cognitive abilities.

It tends to be resistant to conventional teaching methods, but its effect can be mitigated by appropriately specific intervention, including the application of information technology and supportive counseling.

Scotland's working definition

The working definition of dyslexia developed by the Scottish government, Dyslexia Scotland and the Cross Party Group on dyslexia in the Scottish parliament describes dyslexia as:

a continuum of difficulties in learning to read, write and/or spell, which persist despite the provision of appropriate learning opportunities.

The Scottish government adds comment to this definition, stating that:

Dyslexia exists in all cultures and across the range of abilities and socio-economic backgrounds. Learners with dyslexia will benefit from early identification, appropriate intervention and targeted effective teaching.

Dyslexia and the Diagnostic Statistical Manual (DSM-V)

The revision of the Diagnostic Statistical Manual (DSM-V) (American Psychological Association, 2013) uses the term 'Specific Learning Disorder' as a generic term for reading, writing and maths difficulties. This would include dyslexia. DSM-V indicates that the diagnosis requires evidence of persistent difficulties in reading, writing, arithmetic or mathematical reasoning skills during formal years of schooling. Symptoms may include:

- inaccurate or slow and effortful reading
- poor written expression, which lacks clarity
- difficulties remembering number facts, or inaccurate mathematical reasoning.

Implications of the different definitions of dyslexia

While there are different definitions of dyslexia, it is important that this should not in any way undermine the concept of dyslexia. For individuals who have dyslexia the concept is very real indeed. In our practice as psychologists, we have come across countless numbers of children and young people (and parents) who are indeed very frustrated at dyslexia not being taken seriously. For most, it is a serious condition and one that can have a serious impact on the future education, career choice and work opportunities of young people. A diagnosis is therefore very important. It is our view that dyslexia is not represented by a single entity and is in fact multifaceted. When one examines the research it is clear that all these different dimensions have been well researched and although some are more prominent than others, all are important and can impact on the individual's learning opportunities.

Neurological

There is now considerable evidence that there is a neurological basis to dyslexia. This means that the brain structure and the neural connections needed for processing information may develop differently in dyslexic children. Dyslexia therefore should be seen as a difference and not a deficit. This means that children and adults with dyslexia will learn differently and find some types of processing tasks, such as those involving reading at speed and holding information while carrying out another activity, more challenging than many other learners.

Essentially there are two hemispheres in the brain – the left and the right – and generally speaking each hemisphere is more specialised at processing certain types of information. In processing any type of information we use many different parts of our brain. Usually the left hemisphere is mainly responsible for processing language and detailed information, such as decoding print. This means the left hemisphere is important for tasks that are necessary for accurate reading.

The right hemisphere tends to process information that incorporates more holistic information. This would involve visual stimuli and the whole picture – the right hemisphere would process the whole rather than the parts. The right hemisphere usually deals with comprehension and some of the aesthetic aspects, such as art and music. Some neuro-psychologists, such as Bakker (Robertson and Bakker, 2002), have related this to reading and have suggested that right hemisphere readers can become 'sloppy' readers, but may have good comprehension. This can have implications for assessment and particularly identifying the individual's strengths.

There are research activities in different aspects of neurology/brain structure, neurological processing, the cerebellum and the visual cortex, as well as speech and language processing and the processes involved in learning. Cognitive psychologists are involved in studies involving memory and dyslexia as well as the role of processing speed and the cognitive routes to literacy acquisition.

Cognitive – phonological skills

It is often the case that while pupils and students with dyslexia can show skills in right hemisphere processing, they may have difficulty in processing information using the left hemisphere. The skills necessary for accurate reading tend to be left hemisphere skills, such as the skills needed to discriminate different sounds in words. These mostly phonological skills are essential for identifying the clusters of letters that make certain sounds such as 'ough' as in 'tough' and 'ight' as in 'right'. It is now widely accepted that pupils with dyslexia have a weakness in phonological skills and this will certainly affect their ability to read fluently, especially in young readers. There is however evidence that if intervention to teach phonological skills takes place at an early age, the acquisition of literacy can become more accessible (Rose, 2009; National Reading Panel, 2000).

Assessment process – summary

As noted during the course of the book, assessment for dyslexia is a holistic process and one that involves management, teachers, specialist teachers, other specialists, parents and, of course, the individual pupil or student. Additionally, assessment should be 'ongoing' and the results of an assessment should inform practice.

Assessment should therefore be seen as:

1. information gathering

2. interactive

3. informative

4. diagnostic

5. providing a lead into teaching approaches

6. help with the future planning of learning

7. a vehicle to monitor and review progress

8. ongoing so that progress can be monitored and maintained.

We have indicated clearly throughout this book that the assessment process needs to refer to background information as well as the individual's current performances within the curriculum, and that for secondary school students information from all subject teachers needs to be obtained.

Standardised tests also need to be used and, as indicated in Chapter 4 and Chapter 5 (page 50), these tests need to be well standardised and appropriate for the purpose. Testing can be diagnostic and the results of one test should help to decide if and what subsequent tests may be used.

It is a good idea to have a baseline test and this has also been referred to in Chapter 4 (page 38). Psychologists would tend to use the Wechsler Intelligence Scale for Children (WISC-V) and this helps to provide a profile. Weaknesses in this profile – or indeed strengths – can be explored further, either through further testing or through consultancy with the teacher. Teacher assessors can use the Wechsler Individual Achievement Test (WIAT-II-T) and also the Word Identification and Spelling Test (WIST) (see Chapter 7, page 88). The use of the WIST can also help to inform intervention by identifying pupils who are weak in certain aspects of reading and spelling. The WIST can be used diagnostically and this can be its strength. Additionally, it can provide baseline information, and therefore subsequent testing can help to monitor progress.

Some principles of assessment

Some general principles can be noted in carrying out an assessment.

- **Background information:** We have indicated in Chapter 1 the type of background information that is necessary prior to an assessment and this is very important. A pre-assessment interview with the parents of school-aged children is also crucial. This is important for both an in-school assessment and an assessment from an external agency.
- **Formal assessment:** It is important that a lack of availability of a test or tester does not prevent an individual's dyslexic difficulties from being recognised.
- **Informal assessment:** Many of the characteristics can be quite obvious in the classroom situation; it is important that teachers have an understanding of dyslexia in order that these characteristics can be recognised.
- **Appropriate materials and teaching programmes:** These need to be developed from the results of the assessment.

Planning

Planning for learning is important to ensure that differentiation is in place and the child's targets are appropriate and can be met. Some of the key points are highlighted below.

- **Knowledge of the individual's strengths and difficulties:** This is essential, especially since not all pupils or students with dyslexia will display the same profile. This is therefore the best starting point as often strengths can be used to help deal with the weaknesses. For example, dyslexic students often have a preference for visual and kinaesthetic learning and a difficulty with auditory learning. Therefore phonics, which relies heavily on sounds and therefore the auditory modality, needs to be introduced together with visual and experiential forms of learning. The tactile modality, involving touch and feeling the shape of letters, should also be utilised, as well as the visual symbol of these letters and letter/sound combinations.
- **Whole-school approach:** The responsibility for dealing with pupils with dyslexia within the classroom should not solely rest with the class teacher. Ideally it should be seen as a whole-school responsibility. This means that consultation with school management and other colleagues is important, and equally it is important that time is allocated for this. Information from previous teachers, support staff, school management and parents is important and such joint liaison can help to ensure the necessary collaboration to provide support for the class teacher. Importantly, this should be built into the school procedures and not be a reaction to a problem that has occurred – such collaboration can therefore be seen as preventative and proactive.
- **Knowledge of the curriculum content:** It is understood that the teacher will have a sound awareness of the content of the curriculum that the individual needs to know. Anticipating those areas for the different aspects of the curriculum that may present a difficulty for dyslexic pupils may, however, be a bit more tricky. Yet it is important that the teacher can anticipate those areas that may be problematic for dyslexic pupils and students. Such areas can include

information that contains lists or dates, in history, for example. Learning the sequence of dates can be as difficult as remembering the dates. It is crucial therefore that such information is presented in a dyslexia-friendly manner.

- **Current level of literacy acquisition:** An accurate and full assessment of the individual's current levels of attainment is necessary in order to effectively plan a programme of learning. The assessment should include listening comprehension as well as reading accuracy and fluency. Listening comprehension can often be a more accurate guide to the abilities and understanding of dyslexic pupils and students than reading and spelling accuracy. Indeed, it is often the discrepancy between listening comprehension and reading accuracy that can be a key factor in identifying dyslexia. Information on the levels of attainment will be an instrumental factor in planning for differentiation.

- **Cultural factors:** Background knowledge about an individual, particularly cultural factors, is important as this can influence the selection of books and whether some of the concepts in the text need to be singled out for additional and differentiated explanation. Cultural values are an important factor. It has been suggested that the 'big dip' in performance noted in some bilingual pupils in later primary school may be explained by a failure of professionals to understand and appreciate the cultural values and the actual level of competence of the bilingual pupil, particularly in relation to conceptual development and competence in thinking skills. It is possible for teachers to misinterpret bilingual pupils' development of good phonic skills in the early stages of literacy development in English, and they may in fact fail to note the difficulties that these individuals might be having with comprehension. When the difficulties later emerge, these pupils can be grouped inappropriately with native English speakers who have the more conventional problems with phonic awareness, or their difficulties are assumed to derive from specific perceptual problems rather than from the cultural unfamiliarity of the text.

In order for a teaching approach with bilingual students to be fully effective, it has to be comprehensive – which means that it needs to incorporate the views of parents and the community. This requires considerable preparation and pre-planning, as well as consultation with parents and community organisations.

Suggestions for intervention

Some of the key principles of intervention are shown below. These are starting points and will require careful selection of materials and differentiation where appropriate.

Presentation

- **Small steps:** It is important, especially since pupils with dyslexia may have short-term memory difficulties, to present tasks in small steps. In fact one task at a time is probably sufficient. If multiple tasks are specified then a checklist might be a useful way for the pupil to note and self-monitor his or her own progress.

- **Group work:** It is important to plan for group work. The dynamics of the group are crucial and dyslexic pupils and students need to be in a group where at least one member of the group is able to impose some form of structure to the group tasks. This can act as a modelling experience for dyslexic individuals – it is also important that those in the group do not overpower the dyslexic pupil or student, so someone with the ability to facilitate the dyslexic individual's contribution to the group is also important. This would make the dyslexic pupil or student feel they are contributing to the group. Even though they may not have the reading ability of the others in the group, they will almost certainly have the comprehension ability, so will be able to contribute if provided with opportunities.

- **Learning styles:** This is one of the key aspects in understanding the importance of the presentation of materials and how the learning situation can be manipulated to promote more effective learning. It is important to recognise that different individuals will have their own preferred learning style, and this will include dyslexic pupils and students. This means that there may be a great deal of similarities in how pupils and students with dyslexia learn and process information, but there will also be individual differences and these need to be taken into account in the planning and presentation of learning.

Information processing

Learning depends on how efficiently and effectively individuals process information. It is important therefore to recognise the key stages of information processing and how these may present potential difficulties for learners with dyslexia. It is important to recognise how these potential difficulties can be overcome with forward planning and recognition of these in teaching. Some suggestions for this are shown below:

Input

- Identify the student's preferred learning style, particularly visual, auditory, kinaesthetic or tactile preferences, as these can be crucial in how information is presented. It is important to present new information to the learner's preferred modality.

- Present new information in small steps – this will ensure that the short-term memory does not become overloaded with information before it is fully consolidated.

- New material will need to be repeatedly presented through over-learning. This does not mean that the repetition should be in the same form – rather, it is important that it should be varied using as wide a range of materials and strategies as possible.

- It is a good idea to present the key points at the initial stage of learning new material. This helps to provide a framework for the new material and can help to relate new information to previous knowledge.

Cognition

- Information should be related to previous knowledge. This ensures that concepts are developed and that the information can be placed into a learning framework, or schema, by the learner. Successful learning is often due to efficient organisation of information. It is important therefore to group information together and to show the connection between the two. For example, if the topic to be covered was the Harry Potter series of books, then concepts such as witchcraft and magic and the words associated with these would need to be explained and some of the related ideas discussed. This should be done prior to reading the text.

- Some specific memory strategies, such as mind mapping and mnemonics, can be used to help the learner remember some of the key words or more challenging ideas. This can be done visually through mind mapping.

Output

- Often, pupils or students with dyslexia have difficulty identifying the key points in new learning or in a text. This can be overcome by providing the individual with these key points or words at the beginning stage of learning the new material. Additionally, the learner can acquire skills in this by practising using summaries. Each period of new learning should be summarised by the learner – this in itself helps to identify the key points.

- It may also be beneficial to measure progress orally rather than in written form, particularly in-class continuous assessment. It is not unusual for pupils and students with dyslexia to be much more proficient orally than in written form. Oral presentation of information can therefore help to instil confidence. By contrast, often a written exercise can be damaging in terms of confidence, unless considerable preparation and planning have helped to ensure that some of the points indicated above are put into place.

Further tips for supporting learning

One of the key points about intervention is that teaching children with dyslexia is not only about locating and using programmes and off-the-shelf materials. All teaching needs to be contextualised and individualised and this is important when selecting materials. Some suggestions for materials are shown below.

Materials

- **Use of coloured paper:** There is some evidence that different colours of background and font can enhance some individuals' reading and attention.

- **Layout:** The page layout is very important and this should be visual but not overcrowded. Coloured backgrounds are also usually preferable. Font size can also be a key factor and this should not be too small. In relation to the actual font itself, Century Gothic is seen by Dyslexia Scotland as a dyslexia-friendly font (Dyslexia Scotland, 2011).

Tasks

- **Provide a tick list:** This can help to keep the pupil or student with dyslexia on track. It will also help him or her to monitor progress.

- **Breaking tasks into manageable chunks:** This can provide an opportunity for the learner to achieve. Pupils and students with dyslexia can have a low self-esteem. This is because they are in a position of potential failure at school, as most learning is based on print. It is crucial therefore that they achieve and can realise that they have achieved with some tasks. It is this achievement that provides the success needed to raise their self-esteem.

- **Oral feedback:** It is often a good idea to get dyslexic pupils and students to provide oral feedback for the task they have to do. This ensures they have understood the task. At the same time, it is important that the teacher provides oral feedback to dyslexic individuals on how they have managed the task. Oral feedback can be more effective than written comments.

Planning

- **Provide a sequence to help with planning:** Dyslexic pupils and students often have difficulties in developing and following an appropriate sequence. It can be useful to provide a structure that helps to sequence learning of new material. For example, a reading task in which the aim is for pupils to provide a summary of the key points in the passage can be too demanding a task for the dyslexic learner. It is important therefore that the task is broken down into manageable chunks but that there is a clear sequence for the learner to follow, e.g.

1. Underline the important words in the passage.

2. Write them out on a separate page.

3. Then write the meaning of each word next to it.

4. Take one word at a time and indicate why it is important for the passage.

5. Once you have completed this, decide which word is the most important and say why.

6. Give a summary of the key points in the passage.

- **Help the learner to prioritise his or her work:** Often, dyslexic students have difficulty in prioritising their work. This can lead to them spending a lot of time on unimportant areas of the task. It can be a good idea to indicate what aspects of the task are 'very important', 'quite important' and 'less important'.

Writing

- **Writing frames and key words:** Pupils and students with dyslexia need a structure to help them write more fully in written expression. The use of writing frames can help with this. Writing frames can help comprehension and provide a framework for writing.

For pupils and students with dyslexia who have a slow writing speed and perhaps reluctance to write a lengthy piece, it is helpful to provide a framework for the written piece as well as the key words that are to be used. This can speed up the writing process.

- **Unusual writing grip or writing posture:** Special adapted pencils with rubber/spongy grips can help. It is also important to recognise the importance of good posture when writing.

Reading

- **Alphabet games and colour-coding the alphabet:** A pupil or student with dyslexia may have difficulty with the sequence of the alphabet. This can make using a dictionary very time-consuming and frustrating. There are some alphabet games that can be used to help with this. The colour-coding of groups of letters can also be helpful. The alphabet can be divided into seven sections and a different colour for each section.

- **Pronouncing multisyllabic words:** A student with dyslexia may have difficulty pronouncing multisyllabic words, even words that would be common for older students, such as 'preliminary', 'governmental' and 'necessity'. Some voice-activated technology can help with this but if this is not available the child can use a dictaphone and practise saying the word.

- **Slow and hesitant reading:** Reading speed tends to be slow and hesitant and often with little expression for learners with dyslexia. This can happen because pupils and students with dyslexia spend a great deal of effort on reading accuracy. This can result in a loss of emphasis on meaning and expression. The books by Barrington Stoke (www.barringtonstoke.co.uk), which are high interest and have a lower level of vocabulary, can be useful for this.

- **Encouraging reading for pleasure:** It is important that reading takes place every day, even if it is only magazines. Pupils and students with dyslexia might be reluctant to read for pleasure. It is important for the reader to choose his or her own materials.

Spelling

- **Difficulty in spelling:** It is important to look for difficulty in spelling such as: remembering spelling rules; making phonological errors in spelling, for example 'f' for 'ph'; letters being out of sequence; inconsistent use of some letters with similar sounds such as 's' and 'z'; difficulty with word endings, such as using 'ie' for 'y'; confusion or omission of vowels; difficulty with words with double consonants, such as 'commission'.

Memory

- **Poor short-term and working memory intervention:** This will be needed for individuals who have difficulty remembering lists of information – even short lists or short instructions.
- **Strategies to categorise information:** Pupils and students with dyslexia may also show signs of poor long-term memory or have organisational difficulties. The use of strategies to categorise information will make recall easier and strengthen long-term memory.

Movement

Some pupils with dyslexia may have a difficulty with coordination and tasks such as tying shoelaces. They may bump into furniture in the classroom, trip and fall frequently. Some of the factors associated with coordination difficulties can provide clues in the early identification of dyslexia as these factors can often be noted at the pre-school stage. Try to make the classroom environment uncluttered to minimise this problem.

Some key points made in this book

- It is important to have a clear framework for the assessment of dyslexia – a systematic approach to assessment can play a key role in spotting dyslexic indicators that might otherwise have been missed.
- Assessment should be seen as an ongoing process, rather than a one-off screening exercise (although screening can play a role), and the nature of the process will vary according to the age and stage of the pupil or student.
- If dyslexia is identified and accommodated in the early years, it is more likely to become normalised in the classroom environment, and this can be beneficial to the dyslexic pupil's self-esteem.
- Screening should be seen as a filtering process that can play a part in the identification of difficulties, but that should never prevent a pupil or student from access to other forms of assessment at a later date.
- There are some key principles that should form the foundation for all assessments for dyslexia – the first is that assessment should be strengths-based. This is very important, because this provides the information needed to produce recommendations for optimising that person's performance.

- Assessment needs to have a clear aim and purpose and it is important that assessment is seen as a process.
- It is very important that parents should have the opportunity to ask questions, and that they are kept informed of any further assessment that might take place.
- It is important to consider cognitive factors such as working memory and processing speed when assessing for dyslexia.
- Assessment of dyslexia is a process that involves more than using a test.
- The assessment process needs to consider the strengths, difficulties, discrepancies and differences that the child displays.
- Teachers can develop and conduct diagnostic phonological assessment that is contextualised for the classroom.
- Assessment of reading, spelling and expressive writing should also be diagnostic.
- Learning preferences and learning differences need to be taken into account.
- Assessment must have a clear link to intervention.
- It is widely acknowledged that dyslexia can occur across languages, cultures, socio-economic status, race and gender.
- An assessment should involve the parents and carers and should include information on the nature of the individual's language experience and learning opportunities.
- It is important to give feedback to the individual following an assessment.
- Curriculum assessment provides opportunities for teachers to become 'reflective practitioners'.
- An assessment should highlight the learner's strengths and support learners in the development of their learning skills and capacities.

It is significant to end this final chapter on a positive note – indicating that assessment for dyslexia is not only about identifying weaknesses and challenges, but also about highlighting the learner's strengths and providing the means of making positive information available that can help the learner become independent and motivated throughout their school education and beyond, into tertiary education and the workplace.

PART 4

Appendices

Appendix 1
Pre-assessment questionnaires

Pre-assessment questionnaire: parent/carer

Date	
Name of pupil/student	
Name of person completing the form	
Relationship to pupil/student	
What are the pupil's/student's interests at home?	
Does he/she like reading at home?	
What kind of writing activities does he/she prefer?	
What aspects of school does he/she like?	
What aspects of school does he/she dislike?	
Has he/she ever had difficulties with hearing?	*If yes, please describe*
Does he/she have difficulties with hearing now?	*If yes, please describe*
Has he/she ever had difficulties with eyesight?	*If yes, please describe*
Does he/she have difficulties with eyesight now?	*If yes, please describe*
Has he/she ever had difficulties with speech development?	*If yes, please describe*
Does he/she have difficulties with speech now?	*If yes, please describe*
Has he/she ever had difficulties with coordination?	*If yes, please describe*
Does he/she have difficulties with coordination now?	*If yes, please describe*
Does he/she seem more tired than normal after school?	
Is he/she willing and able to do homework independently?	
Does he/she have extra tuition outside of school?	
Has he/she expressed any views about his/her abilities?	*If yes, please describe*
What are his/her strong points?	
Would you like any information from the school?	

Pre-assessment questionnaire: pupil/student

Date	
Name	
What are your favourite activities?	
What is it about these activities that you like?	
Do you like reading?	
What kind of things would you prefer to read?	
Do you ever feel that words, or the gaps between the words, seem to move on the page?	
Do you often skip a word or a line, or read the same word or line twice by mistake?	
Do you like writing?	
Do you feel that you can express your ideas in writing?	
How would you describe your handwriting?	
Would you prefer to handwrite or to use a computer?	
What aspects of school do you like?	
What aspects of school do you dislike?	
Do you find schoolwork tiring?	
Do you find homework manageable?	
What are your strong points?	

Pre-assessment questionnaire: teacher

Date	
Name of pupil/student	
Name of person completing this form	
Role in relation to pupil	
Please describe any difficulties or particular skills you have noted in the following areas:	
Reading – decoding	
Reading – comprehension	
Spelling	
Written expression	
Handwriting	
Following verbal instructions	
Completing work in allocated time	
Concentration	
Memory	
Self-organisation	
Working independently	
Group work	
Consistency of performance	
Other	
What are the pupil's/student's strong points?	

Printable versions of these documents are available at www.bloomsbury.com/reid-guise-dyslexia-assessment

Appendix 2
Assessment consent form

Name of student being assessed: _____

Name of assessor: _____

> *No one will be told anything that you have discussed during the assessment without your permission, except in extreme circumstances, for instance:*
>
> - *if the assessor is concerned for your safety and welfare, or for the safety and welfare of others*
> - *if the assessor is obliged by law.*

I give my consent for an assessment to be carried out. This is to test for learning style, strengths and possible difficulties.

I give consent for information arising from the assessment to be shared with:

Carer/guardian (   )   Tutor/school/college/university (   )

Mother (   )   Workplace (   )

Father (   )   Other: _____ (   )

I give permission for information arising from the assessment, and for any relevant case notes, to be retained by _____ [person] for _____ [time period].

Signed: _____   Date _____

A printable version of this document is available at www.bloomsbury.com/reid-guise-dyslexia-assessment

Appendix 3
The role of professionals

Professional	Function	Access
Practitioner psychologist registered with the HCPC (Health Care Professions Council)	Can administer intelligence tests and other closed tests	Can be through school or privately. Need to ensure they are properly qualified, e.g. in the UK Directory of Chartered Psychologists. Can be consulted via the local public library or the Health and Care Professions Council website: www. hcpc-uk.org
Specialist teacher	Can administer specialised tests that have been developed for dyslexia. Will have knowledge of the implications of the results and what action to take.	Through school.
Class teacher	Can contribute a great deal in terms of information gathered through observation. Will have detailed knowledge of how the pupil performs in class and in different types of activities.	Through school and parents' evenings.
Occupational therapist	Deals with movement and can diagnose specific difficulties in coordination and motor control. Can develop and implement specific exercise-based programmes.	Usually through medical sources or through school.
Optometrist	Deals with visual difficulties, visual acuity, blurring of words when reading and general visual discomfort.	Usually privately, but school can be the first call. Some opticians can provide this service.
Speech and language therapist	Deals with all speech difficulties, articulation, comprehension and associated difficulties.	Through school or medical sources.
Audiometrician	Deals with hearing and discrimination of sounds.	Usually through medical sources, but school may also offer advice.
Neuro-psychologist/ clinical psychologist	Can provide insights if there has been brain or birth trauma and can provide recommendations on programmes that do not necessarily have an educational focus.	Through medical referral.
Occupational psychologist	Can provide guidance on work-based difficulties and recommendations and guidance on career potential and support.	Through employment agencies/employer.

Appendix 4
Teacher's Observation of Learning Styles (TOLS)

(© Reid and Strnadová, 2004)

Social
Interaction
1. Is the student's best work accomplished when working in a group?
Communication
2. Does the student communicate easily with teachers?
3. Does the student like to tell stories with considerable detail?
4. Can the student summarise events well?

Environmental
Mobility
5. Does the student fidget a lot and move around the class frequently?
Time of day
6. Is the student most alert in the morning?
7. Is the student most alert in the afternoon?

Emotional
Persistence
8. Does the student stick with a task until completion without breaks?
9. Does the student require only a little teacher direction in doing the task?
Responsibility
10. Does the student take responsibility for his or her own learning?
11. Does the student attribute his or her successes and failures to himself or herself?
12. Does the student work independently?
Emotions
13. Does the student appear happy and relaxed in class?

Cognitive
Modality preference
14. Does the student readily understand written types of instructions?
15. Does the student readily understand oral types of instructions?
16. Does the student readily understand visual types of instructions?
17. When giving instructions, does the student: • ask for a lot more information? • draw maps (e.g. mind maps)? • take notes?
Sequential or simultaneous learning
18. Does the student begin with step one and proceed in an orderly fashion rather than randomly jump from one step to another?
19. Are the student's responses delayed and reflective rather than rapid and spontaneous?
Tasks
20. Is there a relationship between the student's 'misbehaviour' and difficult tasks?

Metacognitive
Prediction
21. Does the student make plans and work towards goals rather than let things happen as they will?
22. Does the student demonstrate enthusiasm about gaining new knowledge and skills rather than hesitate?
Feedback
23. How does the student respond to different types of feedback, such as: • non-verbal (smile)? • tick mark? • oral praise? • a detailed explanation?
Structure
24. Are the student's personal effects (desk, clothing, materials) well-organised?
25. Does the student respond negatively to someone imposing organisational structure on him or her or with resistance?
26. When provided with specific, detailed guidelines for task completion, does the student faithfully follow them?
27. Does the student seem to consider past events before taking action?

A printable version of this document is available at www.bloomsbury.com/reid-guise-dyslexia-assessment

Appendix 5
Pupil/student Assessment of Learning Styles (PALS)

(© Reid and Strnadová, 2004)

Social
• After school would you prefer to go home in a group or alone?
• Do you like playing computer games with others?
• Do you enjoy working in groups in class?
• Have you got a lot of friends?
• Do you like team games?
• Do you enjoy being with a lot of people?
• Do you like discussing topics in groups?
• Do you like doing your schoolwork with friends or others?
• Do you enjoy spending your weekend with other people?
• Do you see yourself as a leader?
• Are you happy to share your desk with others?

Environmental
• Do you like your desk or work place to be neat and tidy?
• Do you like quiet surroundings?
• Does sound annoy you when you are studying?
• Do you like having lots of space around you when you work?
• Do you prefer to read when sitting at a desk or sitting on the floor?
• Do you prefer light colours (white, yellow) in the room to darker ones (red, dark blue)?
• Do you prefer learning indoors or outdoors?

Emotional
• Do you change your mind about things a lot?
• Do you often feel sad?
• Do you find it difficult to make decisions?
• Do you feel confident?
• Do you worry a lot?

• Do you consider yourself to be reliable?
• Do you often have headaches?
• When you start completing your task, do you finish it?
• Do you consider yourself to have good concentration?

Cognitive
• Do you enjoy doing crossword puzzles?
• Do you remember lists?
• Do you like to learn through reading?
• Do you enjoy picture puzzles?
• Does drawing help you to learn?
• Do you like to use coloured pencils a lot?
• Do you learn best by watching a video or television?
• Do you enjoy experiments?
• Do you learn best by building things?
• Do you learn best through experiences?
• Do you learn best by visiting places?

Metacognitive
• Do you like to make a plan before doing anything?
• Do you usually think how you might improve your performance in any activity or task you have done?
• Do you usually avoid making very quick decisions?
• Do you usually ask a lot of people before making a judgement on something?
• Do you find it easy to organise your ideas?

A printable version of this document is available at www.bloomsbury.com/reid-guise-dyslexia-assessment

Appendix 6
Observation linking assessment and teaching

This can be helpful for developing a learning styles schedule.
(Adapted from Reid and Green, 2016)

Behaviour to be observed	Possible responses	Possible interventions
Attention	Short attention span when listening?	Short tasks with frequent breaks.
Organisation	Keeps losing items – not well-organised?	Needs structure – provide guidance and strategies to help with organisation.
Sequencing	Not able to put things in order or carry out instructions in order?	Make lists, keep instructions short, colour-code.
Interaction	Preferred interaction – one-to-one? Small groups? Whole class?	Try to ensure there is a balance of one-to-one, small group and classwork.
Expressive language	Meaning not accurately conveyed?	Provide key points when discussing. Do not ask open-ended questions. Follow up answers with more specific questions.
Are responses spontaneous or prompted?	Needs a lot of encouragement to respond?	Identify strengths and allow the student to use these in different tasks.
How does the student comprehend information?	Needs a lot of repetition?	Use over-learning but try to make it varied so it is not too repetitive.
What type of cues most readily facilitate comprehension?	Needs a lot of visual cues?	Ensure provision of opportunities for illustrating an answer, e.g. space out work on worksheets – visual image is important; the picture can be annotated, which can indicate if the child has understood.
What type of instructions are most easily understood – written, oral or visual?	Has difficulty with oral instructions?	Ensure instructions are understood – need to be re-inforced verbally.
How readily can knowledge be transferred to other areas?	Has difficulty in knowing how to make connections with previous knowledge?	Needs a structure showing how new learning applies to previous learning.

Behaviour to be observed	Possible responses	Possible interventions
Is the student's reading preference to read aloud or silently?	Has difficulty in reading aloud?	Minimise reading aloud in front of the class.
What types of errors does the student make when reading aloud?	For example, does the child hesitate when reading and omit words?	Paired reading can be useful for this: www.readingrockets.org/strategies/paired_reading
Does the pupil have difficulties in auditory discrimination?	Inability to hear consonant sounds in the initial, medial or final position in a word?	Use paired reading as it provides both auditory and visual feedback to the learner.
Motivation level? Does the student take initiative?	Reluctant to take initiative – needs a lot of prompting and not highly motivated?	Encourage group work in which responsibility is delegated so that everyone has a turn to be in charge.
How is motivation increased – what kind of prompting and cueing is necessary?	Working with others seems to help?	Make sure the group that the student is working in is a positive experience. Experiment until you get the right group dynamics.
To what extent does the student take responsibility for his or her own learning?	Reluctant to do this – needs a lot of coaxing otherwise waits for the teacher to provide instructions?	Meet the student halfway – provide some support and then get him or her to finish it, but ensure there is constant monitoring.
What is the student's level of self-concept? That is, how does the student feel about him- or herself and what are the student's opinions of his or her academic ability?	Seems to have a low self-concept?	Look for ways of giving the student some responsibility for their own learning – identify his or her strengths and highlight these, and try to ensure that tasks are achievable.
What tasks are more likely to be tackled with confidence?	Avoids writing but seems to be confident in practical tasks?	Team the student up with a writing buddy. Balance writing with tactile and kinaesthetic tasks.
Is the child relaxed when learning?	Seems a bit stressed at times?	Avoid too much pressure, e.g. allow more time for tasks – try to ensure that the learner manages to complete all tasks and does not fall behind.
What is the child's learning preferences?	Seems to be visual and kinaesthetic?	Ensure that learning is experiential and that there are a lot of visuals.

A printable version of this document is available at www.bloomsbury.com/reid-guise-dyslexia-assessment

Appendix 7
Record of concern

Name: Date of birth:

Class/tutor group/section:

Concern raised by: Date:

What is the exact nature of the concern?

Details of particular strengths:

Details of any assessments carried out and their outcome:

What support is currently being given and what progress has been made?

What further action is necessary?

A printable version of this document is available at www.bloomsbury.com/reid-guise-dyslexia-assessment

Appendix 8
Checklist on reading and writing

Reading checklist

Sight vocabulary
Sound blending
Use of contextual clues
Attempting unknown vocabulary
Eye tracking
Difficulty keeping the place
Speech development
Motivation in relation to reading material
Word-naming difficulty
Omits words
Omits phrases
Omits whole lines

Writing checklist

Directional difficulty
Difficulty in associating visual symbol with verbal sound
Liability to sub-vocalise sounds prior to writing
Unusual spelling pattern
Handwriting difficulty
Difficulty with cursive writing
Uses capitals and lower case interchangeably and inconsistently
Poor organisation of work on page

A printable version of this document is available at www.bloomsbury.com/reid-guise-dyslexia-assessment

Glossary

ADHD Pupils and students with ADHD (attention difficulties with hyperactivity) will have a short attention span and tend to work on a number of different tasks at the same time. They will be easily distracted and may have difficulty settling in some classrooms, particularly if there are a number of competing distractions. It is also possible for some children to have attention difficulties without hyperactivity. This is referred to as ADD.

Auditory discrimination Many pupils and students with dyslexia can have difficulties with auditory discrimination. It refers to the difficulties in identifying specific sounds and in distinguishing these sounds with other similar sounds. This can be associated with the phonological difficulties experienced by individuals with dyslexia (see **phonological difficulties**). Hearing loss or partial and intermittent hearing loss can also be associated with auditory discrimination.

Cognitive This refers to the learning and thinking process. It is the process that describes how learners take in information and how they retain and understand the information.

Decoding This refers to the reading process and specifically to the breaking down of words into the individual sounds.

Differentiation This is the process of adapting materials and teaching to suit a range of learners' abilities and levels of attainment. Usually differentiation refers to the task, the teaching, the resources and the assessment. Each of these areas can be differentiated to suit the needs of an individual or groups of learners.

Dyscalculia This describes individuals who have difficulties in numeracy. This could be due to difficulties in computation of numbers, remembering numbers or reading the instructions associated with number problems.

Dysgraphia This refers to difficulties in handwriting. Some dyspraxic and dyslexic individuals may also show signs of dysgraphia. Pupils and students with dysgraphia will benefit from lined paper as they have visual/spatial problems and they may have an awkward pencil grip.

Dyslexia This refers to difficulties in accessing print but also other factors such as memory, processing speed, sequencing, directions, syntax and spelling, and written work can also be challenging. Pupils and students with dyslexia often have phonological difficulties, which result in poor word attack skills. In many cases they require a dedicated one-to-one intervention programme.

Dyspraxia This refers to individuals with coordination difficulties. It can also be described as developmental coordination disorder (DCD).

Eye tracking This is the skill of being able to read a line and keep the eyes on track throughout the line. Pupils and students with poor eye tracking may omit lines or words on a page. Sometimes masking a part of a line or page or using a ruler can help with eye tracking.

Information processing This is a process that describes how individuals learn new information. It is usually described as a cycle – input, cognition and output. Often pupils and students with dyslexia can have difficulties at all the stages of information processing, and dyslexia can be referred to as a difficulty or a difference in information processing.

Learning disabilities This is a general term to describe the range of specific learning difficulties such as dyslexia, dyspraxia, dyscalculia and dysgraphia. Often referred to as LD, it is not equated with intelligence, and pupils and students with LD are usually in the average to above average intelligence range.

Learning styles This can describe the individual's preferences for learning; this can be using visual, auditory, kinaesthetic or tactile stimuli but it can also relate to environmental preferences such as sound, the use of music when learning, preferences for time of day and working in pairs, groups or individually. There is a lot of literature on learning styles but it is still seen as quite controversial. This is very likely to be because there are hundreds of different instruments, all of which claim to measure learning styles, and many learners are in fact quite adaptable and can adapt to different types of learning situations and environments. Nevertheless, it is a useful concept to apply in the classroom, particularly for pupils and students with learning disabilities, as, using learning styles, it is more possible to identify an individual's strengths and use these in preparing materials and in teaching.

Long-term memory This is used to recall information that has been learnt and needs to be recalled for a purpose. Many pupils and students with dyslexia can have difficulty with long-term memory as they have not organised the information they have learnt, and so recalling it can be challenging, as they may not have enough cues to assist with recall. Study skills programmes can help with long-term memory.

Metacognition This is the process of thinking about thinking; that is, being aware of how one learns and how a problem was solved. It is a process-focused approach and one that is necessary for effective and efficient learning. Many pupils and students with dyslexia may have poor metacognitive awareness because they are unsure of the process of learning. For that reason, study skills programmes can be useful.

Multiple intelligence First developed by Howard Gardner in the early eighties in his book *Frames of Mind*, it turns conventional views of intelligence on its head. Gardner provides insights into eight intelligences and shows how the educational and the social and emotional needs of all pupils and students can be catered for through the use of these intelligences. Traditionally intelligence has been equated with school success but often this focuses predominantly on the verbal and language aspects of performance. Gardner's model is more broad than that which indicates that the traditional view of intelligence may be restrictive (see Chapter 7, page 81).

Multisensory This refers to the use of a range of modalities in learning. In this context, multisensory usually refers to the use of visual, auditory, kinaesthetic and tactile learning. It is generally accepted that pupils and students with dyslexia need a multisensory approach that utilises all of these modalities.

Neurological This refers to brain-associated factors. This could be brain structure – that is, the different components of the brain – or brain processing – how the components interact with each other. The research into dyslexia shows that both brain structure and brain processing factors are implicated in dyslexia.

Peer tutoring This is when two or more pupils or students work together and try to learn from each other. It may also be the case that an older, more proficient learner is working with a younger, less accomplished learner and the younger one is the tutee and the older one the tutor.

Phonological awareness This refers to the process of becoming familiar with the letter sounds and letter combinations that make the sounds in reading print. There are 44 sounds in the English language and some sounds are very similar. This can be confusing and challenging for pupils and students with dyslexia and they often get the sounds confused or have difficulty in retaining and recognising them when reading or in speech.

Reliability This refers to the reliability in obtaining the same responses from a test if repeated under similar conditions.

Specific learning difficulties This refers to the range of difficulties experienced that can be of a specific nature, such as reading, coordination, spelling and handwriting. There are quite a number of specific learning difficulties and they can be seen as being distinct from general learning difficulties. In the latter case, pupils and students with general learning difficulties usually find most areas of the curriculum challenging and may have a lower level of comprehension than those with specific learning difficulties.

Validity This refers to the design of a test and whether the test actually measures what it was designed to measure, e.g. IQ, decoding, verbal comprehension, etc.

Visual stress Individuals with visual stress have difficulty processing written text. Letters may appear blurred, words may go out of focus or the gaps between the words may appear to move. This can affect comprehension and make reading unpleasant or tiring. Visual stress can be associated with Meares-Irlen Syndrome and Scotopic Sensitivity Syndrome.

Working memory This is the first stage in short-term memory. It involves the learner holding information in their short-term store and carrying out a processing activity simultaneously. This can be solving a problem, reading instructions or merely walking around. Working memory is when one stimulus or more is held in memory for a short period of time. Pupils and students with dyslexia often experience difficulties with working memory as they have difficulty in holding a number of different pieces of information at the same time.

Resources

Dysguise (www.dysguise.com)
Dysguise helps people with learning difficulties to achieve their full potential in life. The company specialises in assessment for dyslexia and other related specific learning difficulties, including dyscalculia (difficulties with numbers), dyspraxia (which includes coordination difficulties) and dysgraphia (difficulties with handwriting). A team of professional associates across Scotland carries out assessments that help people make the most of their skills and realise their learning potential. Dysguise provides full assessments that help identify individual strengths and weaknesses and the particular level of support people might need. This can often be the start of a more positive journey through learning and through life in general. The company's unique model of assessment for children, students and adults offers quality and consistency, and an approach that is also tailored to specific needs.

Dr Gavin Reid (www.drgavinreid.com)
Dr Gavin Reid conducts full psychological assessments in many countries and currently carries out regular independent assessments for schools and centres in Switzerland, Vancouver, Yukon, Cairo, Kuwait, Dubai, Abu Dhabi, Oman, Casablanca, Spain and throughout the UK.

Helen Arkell Dyslexia Centre (www.helenarkell.org.uk)
The Helen Arkell Centre offers dyslexia support and advice. They also offer dyslexia assessments, consultations (for children or adults) and specialist tuition. They provide dyslexia training for teachers and teaching assistants and in-service training for schools and colleges. They have a shop on site and online with books, games and learning resources.

Dyslexia Action Training (Real Group Ltd) (www.dyslexiaaction.org.uk; trainingcourses@dyslexiaaction.org.uk; stuart.curry@realgroup.co.uk)
Holds training courses that are designed to strengthen the expertise and confidence of teachers, SENCos, teaching assistants, instructors, tutors, learning support staff and lecturers who support students with literacy difficulties, dyslexia and other specific learning difficulties (SpLDs).

Institute of Child Education and Psychology Europe (www.icepe.co.uk)
ICEPE Europe (Institute of Child Education and Psychology Europe) is one of the most trusted leading providers of high-quality online continuing professional development (CPD) and university-validated diploma and masters programmes in special educational needs and psychology for teachers, parents and allied professionals who work with children and young people. They offer a wide range of programmes at all levels.

Child Early Intervention Medical Center, Dubai (CEIMC) (http://childeimc.com)
Child Early Intervention Medical Center, Dubai (CEIMC) is a highly specialised centre that focuses on all aspects of child development from birth to 18 years. They offer developmental and psychological assessments, therapy services, special needs support and a variety of programmes for children who require early intervention in learning or behaviour.

The Maharat Learning Center, Dubai (http://maharatlearning.com)
The Maharat Learning Center specialises in dyslexia and associated conditions.

Information and support

Red Rose School (www.redroseschool.co.uk)
Provides for the educational, emotional and social needs of no greater than 48 boys and girls, aged between seven and 16 years.

Dr Sionah Lannen (www.sionahlannen.co.uk)
Based in East Lothian, Scotland, Dr Sionah Lannen conducts assessment for specific learning difficulties, moderate learning difficulties and autistic spectrum disorder.

The International Dyslexia Association (www.interdys.org)
Formerly the Orton Dyslexia Association. Provides resources for professionals and families dealing with individuals with reading disabilities.

British Dyslexia Association (BDA) (www.bdadyslexia.org.uk)
Information and advice on dyslexia for dyslexic people and those who support them.

The Dyslexia Parents Resource (www.dyslexia-parent.com)
Free information about dyslexia, free dyslexia magazine for parents, a free dyslexia advice line, and dyslexia testing.

Dyslexia Association of Ireland (www.dyslexia.ie)
Founded in 1972, the Dyslexia Association of Ireland (DAI) works with and for people affected by dyslexia, by providing information, offering appropriate support services, engaging in advocacy and raising awareness of dyslexia.

Dyslexia Scotland (www.dyslexiascotland.org.uk)
Dyslexia Scotland aims to provide practical help, information and training on all aspects of dyslexia. It seeks to raise awareness of dyslexia and promote good communication between parents and schools. It also runs a helpline open to anyone who has a question about dyslexia and provides information on assessment.

Addressing Dyslexia (http://addressingdyslexia.org)
This free online toolkit is designed for teachers, schools and local authorities, and provides information and guidance on assessing and supporting learners with dyslexia.

Making Sense Review (https://education.gov.scot/improvement/inc37making-sense)
This independent review of education for children and young people with dyslexia was carried out on behalf of the Scottish Government. Its findings and recommendations will help teachers and schools to reflect on the impact of their knowledge and understanding of dyslexia and the support they provide.

DF Optometrists (http://dfoptometrists.com/visual-stress)
DF Optometrists was founded by David Fleischmann, who has ten years' experience in treating and managing visual stress. He works closely with SENCOs to support children and young adults with visual stress and gives talks to local educationalist groups.

The Irlen Institute (http://irlen.com)
The Irlen Institute is the original creator of coloured lens treatment to help manage visual stress and solve associated reading problems. There are over 170 Irlen Clinics across the world.

BRAIN.HE (www.brainhe.com)
Created in 2005, BRAIN.HE aims to provide higher education students and tutors with support and information for all forms of neurodiversity, including dyslexia, dyspraxia, autism and AD(H)D. Its website is an archive of resources and information.

Adult Dyslexia Organisation (ADO) (http://www.adult-dyslexia.org)
The Adult Dyslexia Organisation (ADO) is run by dyslexics for dyslexics and all those concerned with supporting adult dyslexics. ADO not only advises and empowers dyslexic adults, supporting their particular needs, but also offers a range of services to the public and to professionals, service providers and policymakers.

Fun Track Learning Center (www.funtrack.com.au)
Successful learning centre founded and run by Mandy Appleyard in Perth, Western Australia. Their mission statement is 'believing in the potential of every child'.

Centre for Child Education and Teaching (CCET Kuwait) (www.ccetkuwait.org)
The centre aims to champion the inclusion of all individuals with learning disabilities, to develop resources to facilitate the identification of learning disabilities and appropriate intervention, and to provide professional services such as assessment, training courses and short courses on dyslexia and related language disorders.

Useful resources for other specific learning difficulties

SNAP Assessment (www.hoddereducation.co.uk/SNAP)
Award-winning assessment tool to inform on 17 specific learning difficulties. SNAP-SpLD is comprehensive, structured and systematic: it maps each child's own mix of problems onto an overall matrix of learning, social and personal difficulties.

Attention deficit disorders

- The National Attention Deficit Disorder Information Service: www.addiss.co.uk
- Attention Deficit Disorder Association: www.chadd.org and www.add.org
- ADHD behaviour management: www.stressfreeadhd.com
- ADHD books: www.adders.org and www.addwarehouse.com
- ADHD diet: www.feingold.org
- Dyscovery Centre – multidisciplinary assessment centre for dyslexia, dyspraxia, attention deficit disorders and autistic spectrum disorders: www.dyscovery.co.uk

Developmental coordination disorders/dyspraxia

- Dyspraxia Foundation: www.dyspraxiafoundation.org.uk. A UK charity that is actively engaged in a range of activities for dyspraxia, including consultations, conferences and workshops and other awareness-raising events.

Autistic spectrum disorders/Asperger's syndrome

- National Autistic Society: www.nas.org.uk. Comprehensive website relating to all aspects of Autism in the UK.

- www.autismspeaks.org/what-autism. Provides a great deal of information on autism including current research.

Speech and language difficulties

- Afasic: www.afasic.org.uk. Comprehensive website with excellent advice for parents on all speech issues.

- I CAN: www.ican.org.uk. I CAN is a children's communication charity. They help children develop speech, language and communication skills and provide information for parents and professionals.

Bibliography

Aaron, P. G., Joshi, R. M. and Williams, K. A. (1999), 'Not all reading disabilities are alike', *Journal of Learning Disabilities,* 32, 120–137.

American Psychological Association (2013), *Diagnostic and Statistical Manual of Mental Disorders (DSM-V)* (5th edn). Washington DC: American Psychiatric Association.

Bandura, A. (1977), 'Self-efficacy: toward a unifying theory of behavioural change', *Psychological Review,* 84, (2), 191–215.

Barnett, A., Henderson, S. E., Scheib, B. and Schulz, J. (2007), *Detailed Assessment of Speed of Handwriting (DASH).* London: Pearson.

Barnett, A., Henderson, S. E., Scheib, B. and Schulz, J. (2010), *Detailed Assessment of Speed of Handwriting 17+ (DASH 17+).* London: Pearson.

Beery, K. E., Beery, N. A. and Buktenica, N. A. (2006), *Beery-Buktenica Developmental Test of Visual-Motor Integration (Beery VMI)* (6th edn). London: Pearson.

Bell, S. and McLean, B. (2016), 'Good practice in training specialist teachers and assessors of people with dyslexia', in L. Peer and G. Reid (eds), *Special Educational Needs: A Guide for Inclusive Practice.* London: SAGE Publications.

Bowers, P. G. and Wolf, M. (1993), 'Theoretical links among naming speed, precise timing mechanisms and orthographic skill in dyslexia', *Reading and Writing: An Interdisciplinary Journal*, 5, 69–85.

Breznitz, Z. (2008), 'The origin of dyslexia: the asynchrony phenomenon', in G. Reid, A. Fawcett, F. Manis and L. Siegel (eds). *The SAGE Handbook of Dyslexia.* London: SAGE Publications.

British Columbia Ministry of Education (2016), *Special Education Services: A Manual of Policies, Procedures and Guidelines* (section E3). Canada: BC Ministry of Education. www.bced.gov.bc.ca/specialed/special_ed_policy_manual.pdf

British Dyslexia Association, www.bdadyslexia.org.uk/dyslexic/definitions

British Psychological Society (1999), *Dyslexia, Literacy and Psychological Assessment.* Leicester: British Psychological Society.

Bronfenbrenner, U. (1977), 'Toward an experimental ecology of human development', *American Psychologist,* 32, (7), 513–531.

Bryant, B.R. and Wiederholt, J. L. (2011), Gray Oral Reading Test (GORT-5). Pearson.

Burden, R. (1998), 'Assessing children's perceptions of themselves as learners and problem-solvers: the construction of the Myself-As-Learner Scale (MALS)', *School Psychology International,* 19, (4), 291–305.

Burden, R.L. (2002), 'A cognitive approach to dyslexia: learning styles and thinking skills', in G. Reid and J. Wearmouth (eds), *Dyslexia and Literacy.* Chichester: John Wiley.

Burden, R. (2008), 'Is dyslexia necessarily associated with negative feelings of self-worth? A review and implications for future research', *Dyslexia,* 14, (3), 188–196.

Burden, R. (2014), *Myself As a Learner Scale 8–16+: Analysing Self-Perception.* Birmingham: Imaginative Minds.

Burden, R. and Burdett, J. (2005), 'Factors associated with successful learning in pupils with dyslexia: a motivational analysis', *British Journal of Special Education,* 32, (2), 100–104.

Came, F. and Reid, G. (2006), *Concern, Assess and Provide It All!: A Practical Manual for Assessing Individual Needs.* Learning Works.

Carroll, J. M. and Iles, J. E. (2006), 'An assessment of anxiety levels in dyslexic students in higher education', *British Journal of Educational Psychology,* 76, (3), 651–662.

Casserly, A. M. (2013), 'The socio-emotional needs of children with dyslexia in different educational settings in Ireland', *Journal of Research in Special Educational Needs,* 13, (1), 79–91.

Chinn, S. (2012), *More Trouble With Maths: A Complete Guide to Identifying and Diagnosing Mathematical Difficulties*. Oxon: Routledge.

Coffield, F., Moseley, D., Hall, E. and Ecclestone, K. (2004), 'Should we be using learning styles? What research has to say to practice', London: DfES.

Deponio, P., Landon, J., Mullin, K. and Reid, G. (2000), 'An audit of the processes involved in identifying and assessing bilingual learners suspected of being dyslexic: a Scottish study', *Dyslexia*, 6, 29–41.

DfE and Department of Health (2015), *Special Educational Needs and Disability: Code of Practice: 0 to 25 Years*. Crown Copyright.

Dyslexia Action Training (Real Group Ltd), *About Us*, http://www.dyslexiaaction.org.uk/about-us

Dyslexia Scotland (2011), 'Ideas for dyslexia-friendly fonts', www.dyslexiascotland.org.uk/sites/default/files/page_content/DyslexiaFriendlyFonts.pdf

Elbeheri, G. and Everatt, J. (2016), 'Principles and guidelines in test construction for multilingual children', in L. Peer and G. Reid (eds), *Multilingualism, Literacy and Dyslexia: Breaking Down Barriers for Educators*. Oxon: Routledge.

Everatt, J., Ocampo, D., Veii, K., Nenopoulou, S., Smythe, I., Al-Mannai, H. and Elbeheri, G. (2010), 'Dyslexia in biscriptal readers', in N. Brunswick, S. McDougall and P. De Mornay Davies (eds), *Reading and Dyslexia in Different Orthographies*. Hove: Psychology Press.

Everatt, J., Sadeghi, A., Grech, L., Elshikh, M., Abdel-Sabour, S., AlMenaye, N., McNeill, B. and Elbeheri, G. (2013), 'Assessment of literacy difficulties in second language and bilingual learners', in D. Tsagari and G. Spanoudis (eds), *Assessing L2 Students With Learning and Other Disabilities*. Newcastle upon Tyne: Cambridge Scholar Publishing.

Festinger, L. (1957), *A Theory of Cognitive Dissonance*. California: Stanford University Press.

Forbes, S. and Powell, R. (2000), 'Bilingualism and literacy assessment', in L. Peer and G. Reid (eds), *Multilingualism, Literacy and Dyslexia: A Challenge for Educators*. London: David Fulton Publishers.

Frederickson, N., Frith U. and Reason, R. (1997), Phonological Assessment Battery (PhAB) GL Assessments.

Fry, E. (2004), *The Vocabulary Teacher's Book of Lists*. San Francisco, CA: Jossey-Bass.

Gardner, H. (2011), *Frames of Mind: The Theory of Multiple Intelligences* (3rd edn). New York: Basic Books.

Glazzard, J. (2010), 'The impact of dyslexia on pupils' self-esteem', *Support for Learning,* 25, (2), 63–69.

Glutting, J., Adams, W. and Sheslow, D. (2000), Wide Range Intelligence Test (WRIT). Pearson.

Guise, J. and Reid. G. (2016), 'Mind Reading for Teachers: Memory, Metacognition and Effective Learning'. Paper presented at BDA International Conference, Oxford.

Guise, J., Reid, G., Lannen, S. and Lannen, C. (2016), 'Dyslexia and specific learning difficulties: assessment and intervention in a multilingual setting', in L. Peer and G. Reid (eds), *Multilingualism, Literacy and Dyslexia: Breaking Down Barriers for Educators* (2nd edn). Oxon: Routledge.

Heider, F. (1958), *The Psychology of Interpersonal Relations*. New York: Wiley.

HMG (2014), *Children and Families Act 2014*, London: HMSO.

HM Inspectorate of Education (2008), *Education for Learners with Dyslexia*, Scottish Executive. Crown Copyright.

Humphrey, N. (2003), 'Facilitating a positive sense of self in pupils with dyslexia: the role of teachers and peers', *Support for Learning,* 18, (3), 130–136.

Humphrey, N. and Mullins, P. M. (2002), 'Self-concept and self-esteem in developmental dyslexia', *Journal of Research in Special Educational Needs,* 2, (2), 1–13.

Joshi, R. M. and Aaron, P. G. (2008), 'Assessment of literacy performance based on the componential model of reading', in G. Reid, A. Fawcett, F. Manis and L. Siegel (eds), *The SAGE Dyslexia Handbook*. London: SAGE.

Keith, R. W. (2009), *SCAN-3:C Tests for Auditory Processing Disorders for Children*. Pearson.

Kelly, K. (2002), 'Multilingualism and dyslexia'. Paper presented at Multilingual Conference, IDA, Washington, DC.

Kirby, A. and Drew, S. (2017), *Guide to Dyspraxia and Developmental Co-ordination Disorders*. London: Dyspraxia Foundation.

Kirby, A. and Rosenblum, S. (2008), *The Adult Developmental Co-ordination Disorder/Dyspraxia Checklist (ADC) for Further and Higher Education*. Newport, Wales: The Dyscovery Centre.

Landon, J. (2001), 'Inclusion and dyslexia – the exclusion of bilingual learners?' in L. Peer and G. Reid (eds), *Dyslexia and Successful Inclusion in the Secondary School*. London: David Fulton.

Long, L., MacBlain, S. and MacBlain, M. (2007), 'Supporting students with dyslexia at the secondary level: an emotional model of literacy', *Journal of Adolescent and Adult Literacy*, 51, (2), 124–134.

Long, R. and Weedon, C. (2017), *SNAP-Behaviour*. London: Hodder Publications.

Macintyre, C., (2009), *Dyspraxia 5-14: Identifying and Supporting Young People with Movement Difficulties*. London: David Fulton Publications.

Macintyre, C. (2012), *Dyspraxia 5–14: Identifying and Supporting Young People With Movement Difficulties* (2nd Ed). Oxon: Routledge.

Macintyre, C. and McVitty, K. (2004), *Movement and Learning in the Early Years: Supporting Dyspraxia (DCD) and Other Difficulties*. Oxon: SAGE Publishing.

Mahfoudhi, A. and Haynes, C. W. (2009), 'Phonological awareness in reading disabilities remediation: some general issues', in G. Reid (ed), *The Routledge Dyslexia Companion*. Oxon: Routledge.

Malpas, M. D. (2017), *Self-fulfilment with Dyslexia: A Blueprint for Success*. London: Jessica Kingsley Publishers.

Martin, N. and Brownwell, R. (2005), *TAPS-3 Test of Auditory Processing Skills*, (3rd edn). Ann Arbor Publishers.

Miles, T. R. (1996), 'Do dyslexic children have IQs?', *Dyslexia*, 2, (3), 175–178.

Mischel, W. (1973), 'Toward a cognitive social learning reconceptualization of personality', *Psychological Review*, 80, (4), 252–283.

Molfese, V. J., Molfese, D. L., Barnes, M. E., Warren, C. G. and Molfese, P. J. (2008), 'Familial predictors of dyslexia: evidence from preschool children with and without familial dyslexia risk', in G. Reid, A. Fawcett, F. Manis, and L. Siegel (eds), *The SAGE Handbook of Dyslexia*. London: SAGE Publications.

Nalavany, B. A., Carawan, L. W. and Brown, L. J. (2011), 'Considering the role of traditional and specialist schools: do school experiences impact the emotional well-being and self-esteem of adults with dyslexia?' *British Journal of Special Education*, 38, (4), 191–200.

National Reading Panel (2000), *Teaching Children to Read: An Evidence-based Assessment of the Scientific Research Literature on Reading and its Implications for Reading Instruction*. Washington, DC: National Institute of Child Health and Human Development.

Protopapas, A., Fakou, A., Drakopoulou, S., Skaloumbakas, C., Mouzaki, A. (2013), 'What do spelling errors tell us? Classification and analysis of errors made by Greek schoolchildren with and without dyslexia', *Reading and Writing*, 26, (5), 615–646.

Reid, G. (2005), *Dyslexia and Inclusion: Classroom Approaches for Assessment, Teaching and Learning*. Oxon: Routledge.

Reid, G. (2011), *Dyslexia: A Complete Guide for Parents*. London: Wiley.

Reid, G. (2016), *Dyslexia: A Practitioner's Handbook* (5th edn). London: Wiley.

Reid, G. (2017), *Dyslexia in the Early Years: A Handbook for Practice*. London: Jessica Kingsley Publishers.

Reid, G. and Fawcett, A. (2004), *Dyslexia in Context: Research, Policy and Practice*. London: Wiley.

Reid, G. and Green, S. (2016), *100 Ideas for Primary Teachers: Supporting Children with Dyslexia*, London: Bloomsbury.

Reid, G. and Strnadová, I. (2004), *Teacher Observation of Learning Styles (TOLS)*, Collaborative joint project, Charles University Prague and University of Edinburgh.

Reid, G., Green, S. and Zylstra, C. (2008), 'The role of parents', in G. Reid, A. Fawcett, F. Manis, and L. Siegel (eds), *The SAGE Handbook of Dyslexia*. London: SAGE Publications.

Reid, G., Elbeheri, G. and Everatt, J. (2016), *Assessing Children with Specific Learning Difficulties: A Teacher's Practical Guide*. Oxon: Routledge.

Reid Lyon, G. (2004), 'Dyslexia in the USA'. Keynote presentation at the BDA Conference, April 2004.

Riddick, B., Sterling, C., Farmer, M. and Morgan, S. (1999), 'Self-esteem and anxiety in the educational histories of adult dyslexic students', *Dyslexia,* 5, (4), 227–248.

Robertson, J. and Bakker, D. J. (2002), 'The balance model of reading and dyslexia', in G. Reid and J. Wearmouth (eds), *Dyslexia and Literacy: Theory and Practice*. Chichester: John Wiley & Sons.

Rose, J. (2006), *Independent Review of the Teaching of Early Reading* (Rose Report). London: Department for Education and Skills.

Rose, J. (2009), *Identifying and Teaching Children and Young People with Dyslexia and Literacy Difficulties: An Independent Report From Sir Jim Rose to the Secretary of State for Children, School and Families.* Crown Copyright.

Rotter, J. B. (1966), 'Generalized expectancies for internal versus external control of reinforcement', *Psychological Monographs: General and Applied,* 80, 1–28.

SASC (2005), 'Assessment of Dyslexia, Dyspraxia, Dyscalculia and Attention Deficit Disorder (ADD) in Higher Education' in *SpLD Working Group 2005/DfES Guidelines.'* London: DfES (Department for Education and Skills) (www.sasc.org.uk/SASCDocuments/SpLD_Working_Group_2005-DfES_Guidelines.pdf).

SASC (2016), *Suitable Tests for the Assessment of Specific Learning Difficulties in Higher Education*. SASC (www.sasc.org.uk/SASCDocuments/REVISED%20guidelines-March%202016%20a.pdf).

Schön, D. (1987), *Educating the Reflective Practitioner*. London: Jossey-Bass.

Scottish Government, *Definition of Dyslexia* (www.gov.scot/Topics/Education/Schools/welfare/ASL/dyslexia).

Seligman, M. E. (1976), 'Learned helplessness: theory and evidence', *Journal of Experimental Psychology,* 105, (1), 3–46.

Shiel, G. (2002), 'Literacy standards and factors affecting literacy: what national and international assessments tell us', in G. Reid and J. Wearmouth (eds), *Dyslexia and Literacy: Theory and Practice*. Chichester: John Wiley & Sons.

Siegel, L. (2016), 'Bilingualism and dyslexia: the case of children learning English as an additional language', in L. Peer and G. Reid (eds), *Multilingualism, Literacy and Dyslexia: Breaking Down Barriers for Educators*. Oxon: Routledge.

Special Education Support Service, *School-Based Assessment* (www.sess.ie/dyslexia-section/school-based-assessment).

Terras, M. M., Thompson, L. C. and Minnis, H. (2009), 'Dyslexia and psycho-social functioning: an exploratory study of the role of self-esteem and understanding', *Dyslexia,* 15, (4), 304–327.

Torgesen, J. K. (1996), 'A model of memory from an informational processing perspective: the special case of phonological memory', in G. Reid Lyon and N.A. Krasnegor (eds), *Attention, Memory and Executive Function*. Baltimore: Brookes Publishing Co.

Torgesen, J. K., Wagner, R. K. and Rashotte, C. A. (1997), 'Prevention and remediation of severe reading disabilities: keeping the end in mind', *Scientific Studies of Reading*, 1, 217–234.

Tunmer, W. E. and Chapman, J. (1996), 'A developmental model of dyslexia – can the construct be saved?' *Dyslexia*, 2, (3), 179–189.

Wagner, R., Torgesen, J., Rashotte, C. and Pearson, N. A. (2013), *Comprehensive Test of Phonological Processing* (CTOPP) (2nd edn). Austin: Pearson.

Wechsler, D. (2016), *Wechsler Intelligence Scale for Children (WISC-V)*. London: Pearson Clinical.

Wechsler, D. and Naglieri, J. A. (2006), *The Wechsler Nonverbal Scale of Ability (WNV)*. New York: Pearson.

Weedon, C., Reid, G. and Ruttle, K. (2017), *Special Needs Assessment Profile (SNAP)*. London: Hodder Education/Rising Stars.

Weiner, B. (1972), 'Attribution theory, achievement motivation, and the educational process', *Review of Educational Research,* 42, (2), 203–215.

Wilkinson, G. S. and Robertson, G. J. (2006), *Wide Range Achievement Test* (WRAT) (4th edn). Florida: Pearson.

Wolf, M. and Reid, G. (2015), 'Intervention and treatment approaches to dyslexia', *Nature Reviews. Special Issue on Dyslexia*, edited by Al Galaburda.

Wolf, M., Miller, L. and Donnelly, K. (2000a), 'Retrieval, automaticity, vocabulary elaboration, orthography (RAVE-O): a comprehensive, fluency-based reading intervention program', *Journal of Learning Disabilities*, 33, 375–386.

Wolf, M., Bowers, P. and Biddle, K. (2000b). 'Naming-speed processes, timing and reading: a conceptual review', *Journal of Learning Disabilities,* 33, (4), 387–407.

Woodcock, R. W. (2011), *Woodcock Reading Mastery Tests*. London: Pearson.

Woods, K. (2016), 'The role and perspectives of practitioner educational psychologists', in L. Peer and G. Reid (eds), *Special Educational Needs: A Guide for Inclusive Practice*. London: SAGE Publications.

Index